Frieda Anderson

fabric
to dye for

Create **72** Hand-Dyed
Colors for Your Stash

5 Fused Quilt Projects

C&T PUBLISHING

Innovate. Educate. Create.

Text copyright © 2010 by Frieda Anderson

Artwork copyright © 2010 by C&T Publishing, Inc.

Publisher: Amy Marson

Creative Director: Gailen Runge

Acquisitions Editor:
Susanne Woods

Editor: Cynthia Bix

Technical Editor: Carolyn Aune

Copyeditor/Proofreader:
Wordfirm Inc.

Cover/Book Designer:
Kristy K. Zacharias

Page Layout Artist:
Kerry Graham

Production Coordinator:
Kirstie L. Pettersen

Production Editor: Julia Cianci

Illustrator: Aliza Shalit

Photography by Christina Carty-Francis and Diane Pedersen of C&T Publishing, Inc., unless otherwise noted

Published by C&T Publishing, Inc., P.O. Box 1456, Lafayette, CA 94549

Library of Congress Cataloging-in-Publication Data

Anderson, Frieda L.

 Create 72 hand-dyed colors for your stash : 5 fused quilt projects / by Frieda Anderson.

  p. cm.

 ISBN 978-1-57120-823-1 (soft cover)

1. Dyes and dyeing. 2. Color in textile crafts. 3. Quilting. I. Title. II. Title: Create seventy two hand-dyed colors for your stash.

 TT853.A53 2010

 746.6--dc22

 2009020111

Printed in China

10 9 8 7 6 5 4 3 2 1

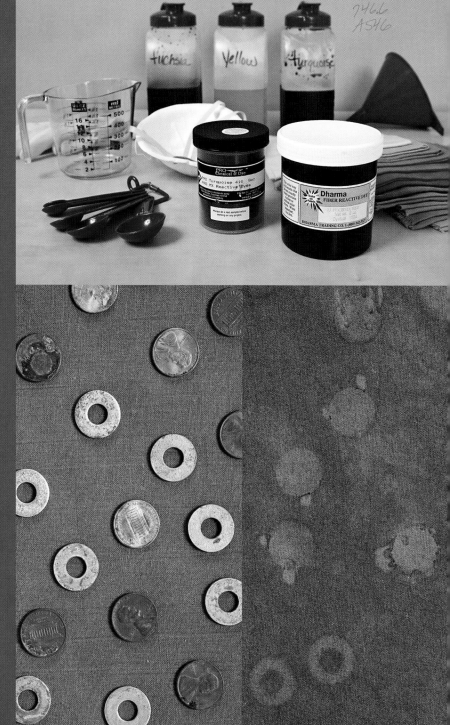

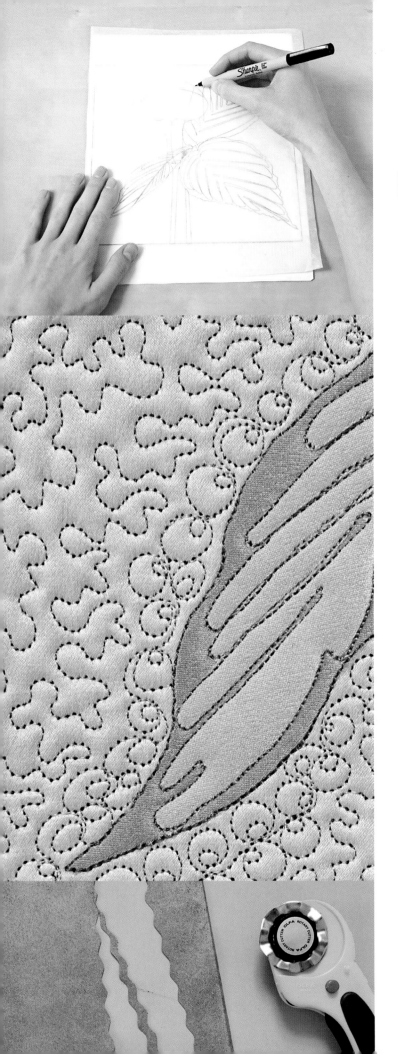

contents

Dedication

I love to quilt, and I love to dye fabric, but if my family were not supportive of what I do, I would never be able to do these things. So I wish to thank my husband, Brett, for being so supportive of my artistic endeavors. He gives me space not only literally, but also figuratively, and he edits all my manuscripts. I couldn't do this without him. I am thankful for my children, Zachary, Lars, and Erik, who think every mother is an artist who has studio space, but especially me.

I wish to thank my mother June, who always encouraged me to be creative and my engineer father Hank from whom I must have inherited the desire to make things.

Acknowledgments

I wish to thank my quilting friends who are there for me every day. Thanks, Laura, Anne, Melody, Emily, Judy, and Ann. Also to PAQA (Professional Art Quilters Alliance) and SAQA (Studio Art Quilt Associates), two groups that help me grow as an artist.

I wish to thank my editor Cynthia Bix for being so supportive and understanding. The writing process needs a lot of fanning of the flames, and Cynthia always sent a gentle breeze my way to keep the fires burning. I also wish to thank all the people at C&T who worked with me on this project. They are so thorough and easy to work with. And thank you to my students who teach me more than I ever teach them.

I am especially thankful for a little dog that came into our lives ten years ago. George is a Jack Russell terrier, and he needs a lot of exercise. If it were not for him needing to get out and run around, I would not take a daily walk in the little, twenty-two acre woods near our home. My daily walks in the woods with George bring to me so much inspiration and information for my artwork. Every day that I enter the woods with George brings me new color combinations and ideas for my quilts. I tell my students that designs and ideas for color combinations are all around us, especially in nature—you only have to look, and I look every day.

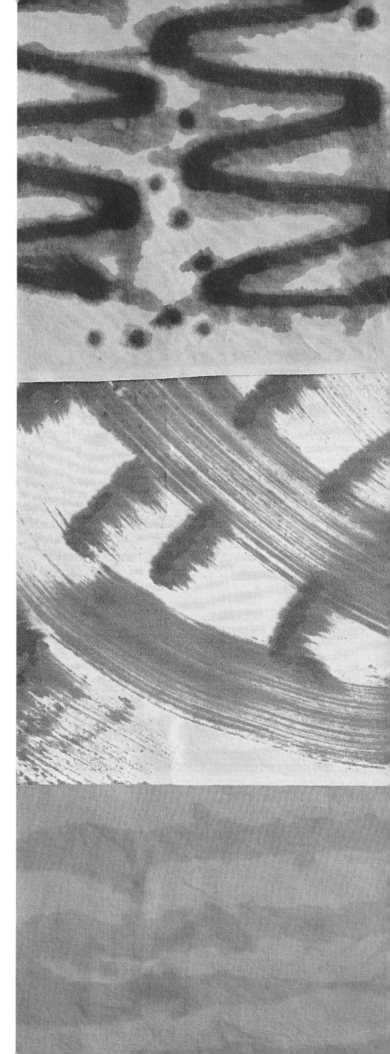

Getting Started

My hand-dyed fabrics

Color is one of the main reasons I love quilting. Because I want to create an abundance and variety of rich, jewel-like colors, I dye my own fabrics.

I started dyeing fabric years ago after I read a magazine article about how to do it. I was inspired, and now I am sharing my accumulated knowledge with you. I hope that you, too, will be inspired to add a wide spectrum of color to your fabric and—ultimately—to your quilts, using this fun and relatively easy method.

I hand dye all my own cotton and silk to use in making my quilts. Even after years of dyeing, seeing the colors emerge on the fabric is still a thrill to me. The process I am going to share with you is easy. It requires only some basic, inexpensive equipment that you can get at any hardware or grocery store; dye powders in basic colors; a place where you can get a little messy; and your own imagination.

This book is written for the first-time dyer. You will learn how to make dye formulas for 72 shades, introducing the flood of color that can be achieved with these dyes. We will dye fat quarters of fabric in various gradations, which are sequences of mixed colors that gradually move from one color to another or from light to dark values of one specific color. In addition to exploring how to achieve colors using basic techniques, we'll also learn special methods such as dyeing fabrics flat and using resists.

We are going to learn to dye the easy way, using ordinary kitchen measuring tools and plastic containers you can find anywhere. With the fabrics you dye, you can create beautiful art quilts using the projects in the book or making up your own. For each project, I will tell you which colors I used.

The only thing standing between you and great hand-dyed fabrics is the "How did she do that?" factor. With this book, you'll soon be saying, "So that's how to do it!"

What are Procion MX dyes?

The most dependable colorfast and wash-fast dyes available are Procion MX Fiber Reactive Dyes, which are the ones used in the instructions and projects presented in this book. They come in powder form and are mixed with water. Fiber-reactive dye is the most permanent of all dye types. Unlike other dyes, it actually forms a bond with the fabric fibers. The fabrics are first soaked in a solution of water and sodium carbonate (soda ash), which changes the pH of the fiber-reactive dye and the cellulose fiber in the fabric. When the mixed dye is used on the presoaked fabric, the dye will bond permanently to the fiber.

I use the Procion MX dyes available from Dharma Trading Company and PRO Chemical & Dye Company. You can find contact information for these companies, as well as for other sources, in Resources (page 79). Some hobby and craft stores also carry these products.

This chart of equivalent colors available from these two companies lists the seven colors we will be using in the gradation dyeing process.

Basic Dye Chart

Dharma Trading colors	Pro Chemical & Dye colors
Bright Color Dyes	
Lemon Yellow #1	#108 Sun Yellow
Fuchsia Red #13	#308 Fuchsia
Turquoise #25	#410 Turquoise
Warm Color Dyes	
Bright Yellow #2	#114 Lemon Yellow
Chinese Red #10A	#805 Mixing Red
Cerulean Blue #23	#406 Intense Blue
Black Dye	
Better Black #44	#608 Black

Dyes

We will start by using the six basic dyes in the Basic Dye Chart plus black to dye the colors in the basic color wheel (see page 13). There are also dozens of premixed dye powders that you can choose from instead of mixing your own. Once you have learned to mix your own dyes using my formulas, you may want to try buying some of the premixed dye colors to play with.

Safety tip

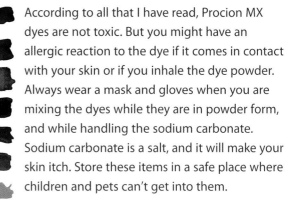

According to all that I have read, Procion MX dyes are not toxic. But you might have an allergic reaction to the dye if it comes in contact with your skin or if you inhale the dye powder. Always wear a mask and gloves when you are mixing the dyes while they are in powder form, and while handling the sodium carbonate. Sodium carbonate is a salt, and it will make your skin itch. Store these items in a safe place where children and pets can't get into them.

Getting Started

What kinds of fabrics work with Procion MX dyes?

Choose 100% plant-fiber fabric such as cotton, linen, Tencel, rayon, or hemp. Silk will also accept color with this process, but in a lighter shade. Fabrics with polyester in them will take some dye, depending on how much polyester is in the fabric. Fabrics that are 100% polyester will not work with fiber-reactive dyes.

"Commercial" fabrics, such as muslin and printed fabrics, that you buy at a fabric or quilt store usually contain starches and finishes that must be removed by prewashing in hot water with laundry detergent before you can dye them; otherwise, the dye will not be well absorbed by the fibers. (Yes, you can overdye commercial print fabrics, as well as white-on-white and black-and-white fabrics—it's fun!)

PFD (prepared for dye) fabrics are the easiest to use, because they are untreated and don't need to be prewashed. You can find PFD fabrics at various supply houses, some of which are listed in Resources (page 79). But once you prewash any fabric, you can treat it just like PFD fabric.

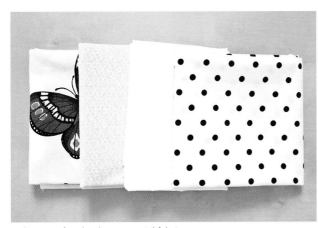

Selection of undyed commercial fabrics

Basic equipment

What's great about this dyeing method is that most of the things you will need are common items that you either already have or can easily get at the supermarket, the drug store, or the hardware store.

Spray bottle, 5-gallon bucket, squirt bottle, quart bottles, small plastic container and lid, dishpan, funnel, measuring cup, and measuring spoons

- A washing machine to rinse out the soaked fabric and to wash out the dyed fabric

- A spray bottle to mist your work surface

- A 5-gallon plastic bucket for mixing sodium carbonate and water—if possible, choose a large plastic container or bucket with a lid.

- A basic kitchen blender for mixing dye with water

Mixing alternative

 A blender really helps the dye to dissolve well. But if you don't want to use one, you can whisk the dye and water vigorously in a small bucket.

- 12 or more plastic food containers. I use the 24-ounce size, because each container can comfortably hold from a fat quarter up to a half-yard of fabric. I prefer containers to ziplock bags because they are stackable, easy to clean, and reusable.

- 12 plastic 1-cup squirt bottles. You can buy these from dye suppliers or beauty shop suppliers, or you can use cake decorating bottles from a craft store. I don't recommend old ketchup or mustard bottles, as the spouts are too large.

- 3 plastic 1-quart wide-mouth bottles with pour lids, like drink containers, to hold the mixed dyes. If you are going to make light gradations, see page 18; you will need 3 additional quart bottles. You can use old milk bottles if you don't want to buy new containers, but a wider opening is easier to pour mixed dye into.

- 2 plastic dishpans—1 to set the blender in and 1 for squishing fabric in. You only need 2, but I have about a dozen, because they come in handy for various jobs.

- A plastic funnel for pouring mixed dye into the quart bottles

- Plastic measuring spoons and cups. I like the spoons that are linked together; they don't get separated, and I can always find the one I need.

Note

The above containers are sufficient for doing one 12-step gradation. There are three 12-step gradations in the Bright Color gradation, and three 12-step gradations in the Warm Color gradation. So, you can either buy 36 containers or wash out and reuse your containers after each 12-step process.

Safety tip

The tools you use should not be the ones you also use in your kitchen! Use your old utensils for dyeing, and treat yourself to new utensils to use in the kitchen. Never use your dyeing tools in the preparation of food, no matter how carefully you have cleaned them.

- Disposable gloves. You can buy these in the pharmaceutical department of a drugstore or at a large discount store. I like them to fit snugly. You can use the big yellow rubber ones, but I find that they fit too loosely.

- A very good dust mask that will not allow dust particles to penetrate, and protective eye gear such as goggles or glasses

- An old apron you don't care about

- Old washcloths or towels cut into rag-sized pieces

Old washcloths, apron, dust mask, goggles, and gloves

- 100% plant-fiber fabric: cotton, linen, Tencel, or rayon. Buy a total of 9 yards of your chosen fabric— 3 yards for each gradation.

Fabric for dyeing

- Sodium carbonate (soda ash) or pH Plus pool supply chemical. You can buy this at your home or building supply store, or through one of the dye companies (see Resources, page 79).

pH Plus pool supply chemical works well to prepare fabric for dyeing.

- A notebook for keeping track of your dye formulas and results

Keeping track

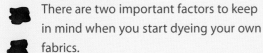
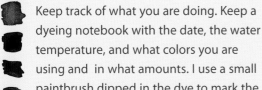

There are two important factors to keep in mind when you start dyeing your own fabrics.

Keep track of what you are doing. Keep a dyeing notebook with the date, the water temperature, and what colors you are using and in what amounts. I use a small paintbrush dipped in the dye to mark the swatches in my notebook; and later I go back and glue a swatch of the dyed fabric on the page as well.

Have fun and experiment! But keep track of your experiments so you can replicate them if you want to, or so you can remember never to try them again!

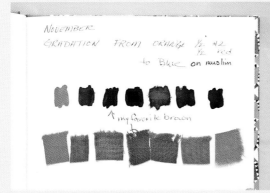

Typical page in my dye notebook

Setting up your workspace

WHEN SETTING UP YOUR DYEING WORKSPACE, KEEP IN MIND THESE HELPFUL TIPS:

- Cover your work surface.

- Keep the dye contained.

- Wear old clothes.

- Keep your hands clean.

Choosing a workspace

To get started, first find a place where you can work safely and where making a mess will not matter—a basement, garage, or utility room, if you have one, where you have access to hot running water. Find the place where you will be most comfortable.

Because you will mostly be standing up, you'll need a work surface such as a counter or table that is at a comfortable working height. You don't want to be bending down all day!

I dye in my laundry room area. I use the top of my washing machine as a surface for mixing dyes. (I protect the top with old towels.) Next to it, I have a table, lifted to a good working height, to spread my fabric on.

For me, the washing machine and a portable folding table put up on lifters are the perfect heights. I use PVC pipe (plastic plumbing pipe) cut to specific sizes to lift my tables (see pages 24–25).

I also have a heavy rubber mat to stand on. Standing on concrete or any other hard surface will make your legs ache after a while. These mats are sold in home supply or hardware stores.

Preparing the dye area

Cover the surface of your washer, counter, or table with materials that can be moistened and either discarded or washed, such as stacked old newspapers or an old blanket or towel.

You will use the spray bottle to moisten the working surface with water. This will keep any spilled dye powder on the work surface, so it doesn't become airborne and migrate to other areas. This is important, particularly if you are working in your laundry area.

My oldest son has asked me to warn you to remove all laundry from the work area. I guess he didn't like having yellow spots on his shirts and underwear! Really, that was the one and only time that I ever got dye on any of my laundry, but it happened because dry dye powder migrated away from my work surface.

Once you are finished mixing the dyes, you can roll up and throw away the old newspapers or wash out the towel or blanket when you wash out your fabrics. It's a good idea to first roll up the towel or blanket to contain any dry dye powder that may have spilled, and carefully empty the towel over a nearby washbasin or garbage can so that you don't scatter dye powder when you move the towel.

Place your blender in one of the dishpans. Then place the dishpan on top of the moistened work area, and plug in the blender.

Placing the blender in the dishpan will help control any spills that might happen while you're mixing the dyes. Remember, you want to keep your work area as clean as possible and the dye contained as much as possible.

Blender in dishpan on dampened towel

Set out the 3 quart-size bottles for the mixed dye, a squirt bottle for the black dye, and the 12 small plastic containers with their lids next to them for the dyed fabrics. Don't forget the measuring cup and spoons.

With a black permanent marker, mark the quart containers "Fuchsia," "Yellow," and "Turquoise." The small plastic containers don't need to be marked because you will mark the fat quarters with numbers to keep track of the dye colors.

Plastic containers and marked quart bottles

Dressing for dyeing

Where dye lands, dye stays! So be sure to wear a set of old clothes when dyeing. I even have dye shoes and underwear, and a dye hat for when I dye outdoors. I have summer dye clothes and winter dye clothes. I also wear a dye apron and keep a dye towel tucked into the tie strings of my apron. That way I don't have to search for a towel, and I always have a handy place to wipe my hands when I'm working.

I also keep a bowl of clean water on my work surface to rinse my hands in so that I don't have to turn the water off and on all the time. You really want to keep your hands clean when working because, remember, where dye lands, dye stays. It won't wash away like food coloring, and if you handle your fabric with dye on your hands, you will have little dots of color in areas where you don't want them.

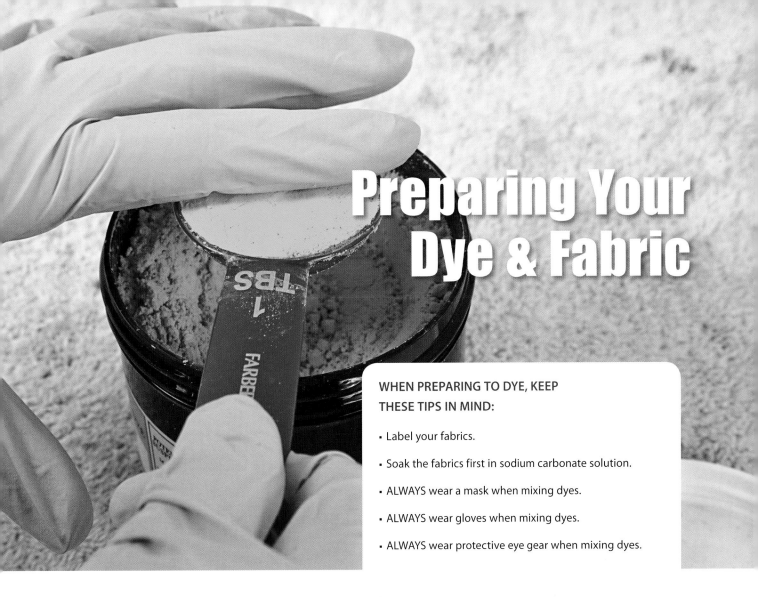

Preparing Your Dye & Fabric

WHEN PREPARING TO DYE, KEEP THESE TIPS IN MIND:

- Label your fabrics.

- Soak the fabrics first in sodium carbonate solution.

- ALWAYS wear a mask when mixing dyes.

- ALWAYS wear gloves when mixing dyes.

- ALWAYS wear protective eye gear when mixing dyes.

You will do three 12-step gradations using the Bright Colors, then three 12-step gradations using the Warm Colors (see the chart on page 6). Of course, you won't do all these in a day; you'll be doing them over time, as quickly or as slowly as you want. You will eventually want to have fabric in all 72 colors available to you for making quilts.

We will start by mixing quart bottles of three basic primary colors—red, blue, and yellow. We'll also mix some black dye. We'll make a medium-value gradation, then a light-value gradation, and finally a blackened-value gradation, all from the 4½ cups each of mixed yellow, red, and blue dyes. At the end, you will have 36 fat quarters of fabric dyed in a rainbow of colors to use in your quilt projects.

Preparing the fixative

To start, fill up the 5-gallon plastic bucket with hot water from the faucet. Mix in ½ cup to 1 cup of sodium carbonate per gallon of water. You will be presoaking the fabrics in this sodium mixture.

This is important. Remember, the sodium carbonate, or soda ash, is the fixative that makes the Procion MX dye bond with the fibers in the fabric so that there is beautiful, permanent color all the way through the fabric fibers.

The fabric should sit in the fixative for a minimum of 5 to 15 minutes, but it can soak longer. I sometimes leave fabrics soaking for days in the buckets until I get around to dyeing them.

Preparing the fabric

If your fabrics are not PFD fabrics, make sure they are prewashed (see page 7).

Now it's time to prepare your fabrics. Start out with at least 9 yards of plain cotton fabric. We will make 3 different 12-step Bright Color gradations, so we need 36 fat quarters or quarter-yards—1 for each gradation.

I usually rip my 9 yards first into 1-yard pieces. Then I fold each piece in half lengthwise and rip it at the fold. Next, I fold each half-yard in half and rip it at the fold to create 4 pieces—or fat quarters—18″ × 20–22″, depending on the width of the fabric. You could also rip each yard into 4 regular quarter-yards if you prefer.

Stack these into 3 piles, or sets, of 12 each. With a permanent marker, mark the corner of each piece in the first set from 1 to 12. Repeat the numbering from 1 to 12 for the other 2 sets of fabric.

Set of twelve numbered fat quarters

Keep each pile in order, with the #1 fat quarter on top and #12 fat quarter on the bottom. To each set, add a letter to the label: L for light, M for medium, or D for dark.

These 3 piles, or sets, should stay together in their stacks throughout the dyeing process.

Place the first pile in the sodium bucket. Push the whole pile down, and soak all the fabric. After 15 minutes, pull the stack up, and let the numbered corners hang over the edge of the bucket. The corners where the numbers are should be at the top of the bucket, sticking out just enough so that you can grab the corner of the fabric.

Mixing the basic dyes

We are now going to start mixing the first set of 3 primary colors—yellow, red, and blue—to achieve our first color wheel gradation: the Bright Color gradation.

> **Note**
>
> In the instructions, I will refer to the Dharma colors, but you can substitute the equivalent PRO Chemical & Dye colors (see the chart on page 6).

Using Lemon Yellow #1, Fuchsia Red, and Turquoise Blue, we will create a 12-step Bright Color gradation, starting with yellow and blending our colors through to lime green. The first 3 dyes will be mixed in the blender, one after the other. You need to have your Better Black dye on hand as well.

Always rinse the blender well between mixing the colors. Even so, I suggest that you work from the lightest to the darkest, mixing the yellow dye first, then the fuchsia, and finally the turquoise. That way, when you move from mixing one dye to the next, the previous color will not affect the next color. You will mix the black dye separately.

Have all the dyes and measuring equipment ready and next to your work area (see Preparing the Dye Area, page 9). The small plastic containers should be open, ready for you to put the fabrics in once you have poured dye over them. Be sure you are wearing a mask, gloves, and protective eye gear.

Now it's time to mix the dyes. The 3 dye mix formulas are as follows:

2 tablespoons of Lemon Yellow #1 + 4 cups of hot water

2 tablespoons of Fuchsia Red + 4 cups of hot water

2½ tablespoons of Turquoise Blue + 4 cups of hot water

Note that because turquoise dye is lighter in weight than the other 2 dyes, you need more to achieve an even color. Later, when you are doing the Warm Color gradation (page 19), 2 tablespoons of the Cerulean Blue will be sufficient.

Smaller Batches

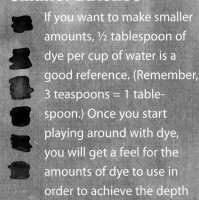

If you want to make smaller amounts, ½ tablespoon of dye per cup of water is a good reference. (Remember, 3 teaspoons = 1 tablespoon.) Once you start playing around with dye, you will get a feel for the amounts of dye to use in order to achieve the depth of color you like.

The color wheel

You can refer to the color wheel to understand how colors blend from one to the next. Consider buying one—they're inexpensive, and a color wheel is a good tool for making color choices in all your quilting projects.

The color wheel shows the twelve pure colors. The three primary colors are red, yellow, and blue. The three secondary colors—orange, green, and violet—are each composed of two primary colors mixed together. The six tertiary (intermediate) colors—yellow-orange, red-orange, red-violet, blue-violet, blue-green, and yellow-green—are each composed of one primary and one secondary color mixed together.

Complementary colors are two colors opposite to one another on the color wheel.

Colors can be "aggressive" or "receding." Aggressive colors are the warm colors—reds, oranges, and yellows. Receding colors are the cooler colors—greens, blues, and violets.

For any color, the value of the color simply refers to how light or dark it is.

A color family is made up of a pure color and all its tints, tones, and shades. A tint is a color with white added to it, a tone is a color with gray added, and a shade is a color with black added.

A color wheel and the C&T 3-in-1 Color Tool are good reference tools for all your quilting projects.

Make sure the water is at least 70 degrees. I use it hot from the tap. If the water gets cold, the dye won't work as well. Once the dye is mixed with the water, it is good for up to 7 days if kept at room temperature or above.

Fill the blender to the 4-cup mark with hot water and place it securely on the motor casement. Remember, work over the moistened towel area in case any dyes are scattered. With dry gloved hands, measure out 1 tablespoon of yellow dye, leveling it off with your finger over the dye container.

Measuring dye

Place the dye in the blender. Measure off the additional tablespoon. (Refer to Mixing alternative, page 7, if you are not using a blender.)

Replace the top on the dye container, and screw it on tightly before you mix the dye. You don't want to get dye powder on anything, so it is important to be very careful at this stage. Secure the top on the blender and blend well for 30 seconds.

Pour the mixed yellow dye into its marked quart container. Rinse out the blender, and repeat the process for the fuchsia, and then for the turquoise dye.

Three primary-color mixed dyes

Now we're almost ready to start the gradation process. But first, we need to mix a batch of black dye to use in the third (dark-value) gradation.

> **Note**
>
> If you are going to do dark-value gradations on a different day, wait to blend the black dye until right before using it.

Place 2 leveled tablespoons of Better Black dye in the blender. Add 1 cup of hot water from the tap. Secure the top on the blender and blend well for 30 seconds. Place the blended black dye in a 1-cup squirt bottle, and set it aside for the last gradation value set.

Mixed black dye

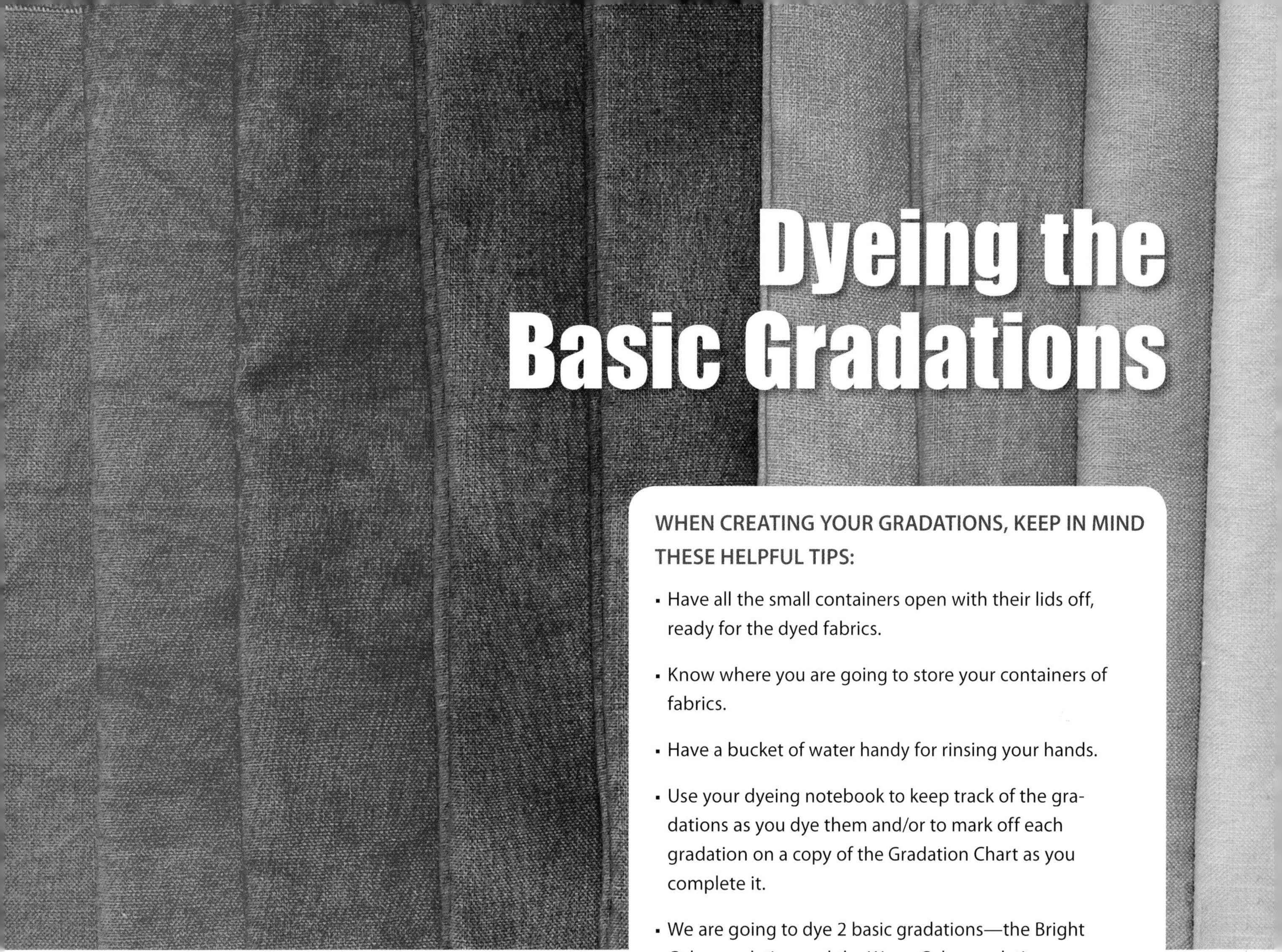

Dyeing the Basic Gradations

WHEN CREATING YOUR GRADATIONS, KEEP IN MIND THESE HELPFUL TIPS:

- Have all the small containers open with their lids off, ready for the dyed fabrics.

- Know where you are going to store your containers of fabrics.

- Have a bucket of water handy for rinsing your hands.

- Use your dyeing notebook to keep track of the gradations as you dye them and/or to mark off each gradation on a copy of the Gradation Chart as you complete it.

- We are going to dye 2 basic gradations—the Bright Color gradation and the Warm Color gradation. Within each of these, we will do 3 different 12-step gradations—a medium-value gradation, a light-value gradation, and a dark-value gradation. The Gradation Chart on this page works for both the Bright Color gradations and the Warm Color gradations.

Gradation Chart

Gradation Step Number	Dye Formula	Color
1	¼ cup Y	Yellow
2	¼ cup Y + 1½ tsp R	Yellow-orange
3	¼ cup Y + ¼ cup R	Orange
4	1 tbsp Y + ¼ cup R	Red-orange
5	¼ cup R	Red
6	¼ cup R + ½ tsp B	Red-violet
7	¼ cup R + ¼ cup B	Violet or Purple
8	1 tbsp R + ¼ cup B	Blue-violet
9	¼ cup B	Blue
10	¼ cup B + 1½ tsp Y	Blue-green
11	¼ cup B + ⅓ cup Y	Green
12	½ tsp B + ¼ cup Y	Lime or Yellow-green

- tbsp = tablespoon
- tsp = teaspoon
- Y = yellow
- R = red or fuchsia
- B = blue or turquoise

Tip

Copy this chart into your dyeing notebook. You will want to mark off the colors as you do them.

Dye proportions

I have found that, in general, 1 cup of mixed dye will dye 1 yard of fabric. So ¼ cup of dye will dye a fat quarter of fabric. This is just a generalization; heavier fabrics, such as velveteen or corduroy, soak up more moisture and require more dye.

Bright Color gradations

Now the fun begins. Have all the dyes in their separate containers, along with measuring cups, spoons, and open containers, set out on your work surface. Keep a bowl or small bucket with clean water on the work surface to rinse your hands between steps in the gradation.

First gradation: medium value

You will start the first Gradation Step with Fabric #1 and the yellow dye.

1. With clean-gloved hands, remove Fabric #1 from the pile of fabric soaking in the sodium bucket. It should be on top. Wring it out well over the sodium carbonate bucket. (If you are dyeing 1-yard pieces of fabric, you might want to wring them all out in the washer on the spin cycle, and place all the wrung-out fabrics in a clean dishpan.)

Pull out first fabric.

2. Place this fabric in a clean dishpan. Measure out ¼ cup of yellow dye—Gradation Step 1 in the Gradation Chart (page 15). Pour the dye over the fabric. With gloved hands, squish it around until the dye covers all the fabric. Do this thoroughly, opening up the fabric and making sure the dye is evenly distributed all over it.

Squish dye through fabric.

3. Squeeze out the extra dye, and put the fabric into a plastic container. It should be thoroughly and evenly saturated with color.

Move dyed fabric to its container.

Bring a friend!

You may be someone who likes to work alone at your own pace. But it's especially easy and fun to dye with friends. I like to have students in my dye classes team up in pairs to make the work go faster and to make it more fun. It also helps to keep everything clean and neat. If you dye with a friend, you can assign a "dirty" person and a "clean" person. The dirty person measures the dye and squishes the dye around once it is poured over the fabric. The clean person handles the undyed fabrics and finds anything that is missing.

Remember that if you are dyeing with a partner, you will each want a quarter-yard of fabric to dye, and you will have to mix extra dye to do all the gradations.

Dyeing the Basic Gradations

Excess dye

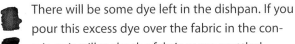

There will be some dye left in the dishpan. If you pour this excess dye over the fabric in the container, it will make the fabric more mottled.

If you don't want to pour it on the fabric, you can have extra fabric waiting in a separate container and pour the excess dye on it (See Using Up Leftover Dye, page 20).

4. Place the lid on the container, and set it aside. Rinse your hands in the rinse bowl, and rinse out the dishpan. The dye begins to lose its strength once it is mixed with the sodium carbonate, so you can't reuse any dye you squeeze out of your samples, even though the color still looks very intense.

5. Now you're ready to move to the second step in the gradation. Take Fabric #2 out of the sodium bucket and place it in the clean dishpan. Measure out and mix ¼ cup yellow dye and 1½ teaspoons red dye Gradation Step 2 in the Gradation Chart (page 15).

6. Repeat Steps 2 through 4 with Fabric #2.

7. Continue the above process with each of Fabrics #3 through #12 in turn, mixing the colors in sequence.

You have now have completed the first gradation in a medium-value dye lot. Set it aside to age for at least 2 hours.

With the 2½ cups of dye that are left, we will do 2 more value gradations.

First gradation waiting to age

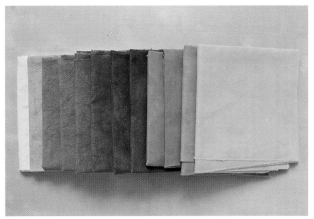
First gradation of colors (medium value)

Mixing dyes

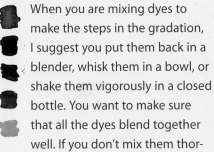

When you are mixing dyes to make the steps in the gradation, I suggest you put them back in a blender, whisk them in a bowl, or shake them vigorously in a closed bottle. You want to make sure that all the dyes blend together well. If you don't mix them thoroughly, the colors will tend to separate on the fabric and look mottled.

Blending dyes with whisk

Mottled dye

Second gradation: light value

The second gradation is a light color value. Have a new pile of numbered fabrics soaking and ready to go in sodium carbonate solution, and have 12 clean small containers and lids ready.

From each of the 3 basic mixed dyes in the original quart bottles—the yellow, red, and blue—measure out ½ cup of dye. Place each color separately into a new quart container. To each container add 2 cups of water. Shake the containers well to mix, or place them back in the blender and mix well. Remember, you don't want splotchy blending of the dyes.

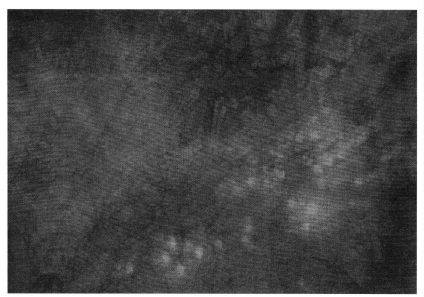

Splotchy blending of colors

Starting second gradation

Use these 3 new basic dyes to dye Fabrics #1 through #12. Simply repeat the steps (Steps 1 through 7) that you followed in the medium-value gradation process.

Tip

You could even go lighter than this value by starting out with only ¼ cup of dye and adding more water. Or, for a really light-value gradation, start out with 2 tablespoons of dye, and add water to make a total of 2½ cups.

Second gradation of colors (light value)

Third gradation: dark (blackened) value

For the third gradation, we will add the mixed black dye to the 3 basic colors. As for the other gradations, have 12 new numbered fabrics soaking in sodium carbonate and ready to go.

Into each of the 3 colors left in the original quart containers, add 2 tablespoons of premixed black dye. Shake the containers well to mix, or place them back in the blender and mix well.

Dyeing the Basic Gradations

Using the blackened dye mixtures, make the third gradation set in the same manner as you did the first 2, following Steps 1–7 on pages 16–17.

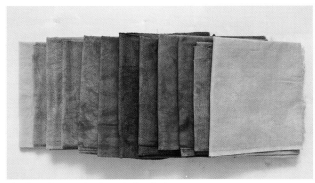
Third gradation of colors (dark value)

Congratulations! You have now completed three value gradations: a medium Bright Color value, a light Bright Color value, and a blackened Bright Color value. We have made this gradation with three Bright Color dyes.

Warm Color gradations

You can repeat the whole gradation process with Warm Color dyes instead of the Bright Color dyes we used in the last sequence. Again, you will make three two-color, 12-step gradations. Use the dyes listed under Warm Color Dyes in the Basic Dye Chart on page 6 and the amounts listed in the Gradation Chart on page 15. If you are using Dharma colors, the dyes will be Bright Yellow #2, Chinese Red, and Cerulean Blue.

Bright Yellow #2, Chinese Red, and Cerulean Blue dyes

You will start out with 36 new pieces of fabric, and you can use the same equipment and containers (all cleaned up, of course) that you used to make the Bright Color gradations. Just like you did for that sequence, you will dye a medium-value gradation, a light-value gradation, and a dark- or blackened-value gradation.

For fun, you can try overdyeing commercial fabrics, including prints and white-on-white fabrics, as well as dyeing plain white fabric.

Warm Color gradations in medium value, light value, and dark value—done on muslin and overdyed commercial fabrics

White-on-white fabrics overdyed in Warm Color gradation

Three values of one color gradation

Once you have completed the Bright Color and Warm Color gradations, you can start experimenting with mixing the colors from both sets of primary colors to achieve completely different varied gradations.

Here are all the yellow/red/blue combinations you can mix from the six basic colors of Yellow #1, Fuchsia Red, Turquoise Blue, Yellow #2, Chinese Red, and Cerulean Blue (see the Basic Dyes chart on page 6).

Using Yellow #1

1. Lemon Yellow #1, Fuchsia Red, Turquoise Blue

2. Lemon Yellow #1, Fuchsia Red, Cerulean Blue

3. Lemon Yellow #1, Chinese Red, Turquoise Blue

4. Lemon Yellow #1, Chinese Red, Cerulean Blue

Using Yellow #2

1. Bright Yellow #2, Fuchsia Red, Turquoise Blue

2. Bright Yellow #2, Fuchsia Red, Cerulean Blue

3. Bright Yellow #2, Chinese Red, Turquoise Blue

4. Bright Yellow #2, Chinese Red, Cerulean Blue

Of course, there are many different yellows, reds, and blues available from the various dye companies. The variations can go on and on.

Write it down

I suggest that when you start playing around with the different variations, you record all your formulas and samples in your dyeing notebook for easy reference (see Keeping Track, page 9). You will want to refer to this when picking out colors that you want to dye with again.

Using up leftover dye

After you have finished your gradations, you may have some dye left over. A great way to use it up is to take a piece of fabric that has been presoaked in sodium carbonate, wring it out, and place it in a dishpan or plastic container. Then just pour the leftover dye on top of it, letting all the colors mix together. I call this "mystery fabric." You can get some wonderful results working like this.

Mystery fabric

Dyeing More Gradations

WHEN CREATING ADDITIONAL GRADATIONS, KEEP IN MIND THESE HELPFUL TIPS:

- Have on hand the same basic equipment that you used for the previous gradations.

- It is helpful to number the fabrics for these gradations as you did the others, so you can tell which one is what step in the blending of colors.

- For the dye formulas, refer back to Dyeing the Basic Gradations, pages 15–20.

- When creating these gradations, your color wheel (see page 13) will come in handy.

- There are other types of gradations that I know you will want to play with. These are more limited in terms of color choice but achieve gorgeous results.

Gradations from complementary colors

For these gradations, you will mix together two complementary colors. (Remember that complementary colors are opposite each other on the color wheel.) For example, you might mix orange with its opposite, blue. The dye colors you use will be the same ones you mixed in Dyeing the Basic Gradations (pages 15–20).

These gradations will give you beautiful muted colors in the middle ranges between the two main colors.

To start, mix 4 cups of each color you will work with—for example, 4 cups of orange and 4 cups of blue—using the dye formulas in the Gradation Chart on page 15.

We will mix 6 different gradations, mixing Color A's with Color B's. The 6 are listed below.

- Orange (A) to blue (B) gradation

- Yellow-orange (A) to violet-blue (B) gradation

- Yellow (A) to violet (B) gradation

- Yellow-green (A) to red-violet (B) gradation

- Green (A) to red (B) gradation

- Turquoise (A) to red-orange (B) gradation

4 examples of gradations from complimentary colors:

Orange-to-blue gradation

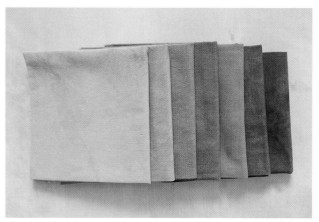

Yellow orange-to-blue violet gradation

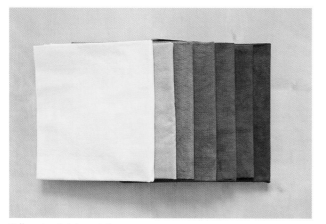

Yellow-to-violet gradation

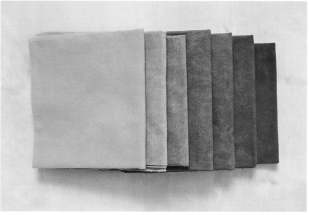

Yellow green-to-red violet gradation

For each gradation, you will follow the 7 Gradation Steps listed in the Complementary Color Gradation Chart shown at the right, using the dye formula that corresponds to each step.

Prepare and presoak the fabric, and dye it in the same way you dyed the gradations in Dyeing the Basic Gradations, pages 15–20.

Complementary Color Gradation Chart

Gradation Step Number	Dye Formula
1	1 cup A
2	1 cup A + 1 tbsp B
3	¾ cup A + ¼ cup B
4	½ cup A + ½ cup B
5	¼ cup A + ¾ cup B
6	1 tbsp A + 1 cup B
7	1 cup B

A = the first color; B = its complement

Color family gradations from dark to light

I know you will want to create gradations within a color family—grading from the full strength of one color to a very pale value of that color. Remember from our earlier discussion of color (see page 13) that a color family is made up of a pure color, such as red, and all its tints, shades, and tones. In this gradation, we're working with tints.

With paint, you would add white to a color to create a tint, but there is no such thing as white dye. Instead, you will create tints by reducing the amounts of dye and increasing the amounts of water.

You will make a gradation of 7 tints of one color, from dark to light. For each tint, set aside a 24-ounce plastic container.

Cut up at least 7 fat quarters of fabric, number them, and presoak them in sodium carbonate solution (see Preparing the Fabric, page 12).

Three dark-to-light gradations: Cerulean Blue, Fuchsia, and Lime Green #12

To begin, mix 3 cups of the pure color you want to start with, such as fuchsia or yellow. You will have enough dye to color up to 1 yard of fabric with each step. With a measuring cup, measure off each step of the dye gradation using the 3 cups of mixed dye.

Single-Color Gradation Chart

Gradation Step Number	Dye Formula
1	1 cup of pure color dye
2	½ cup dye + ½ cup water
3	¼ cup dye + ¾ cup water
4	2 tbsp dye + water to make 1 cup
5	1 tbsp dye + water to make 1 cup
6	1 tsp dye + water to make 1 cup
7	½ tsp dye + water to make 1 cup

Follow the same basic how-to steps you used to make the first basic gradation (see Dyeing the Basic Gradations, pages 16–17). Pull the fat quarter of Fabric #1 from the sodium carbonate solution, wring it out, and place it in a plastic container. Measure out the first Gradation Step formula (1 cup of pure color). Pour the dye over the fabric, and squish it around.

Repeat this process for each Gradation Step in the chart above, using Fabrics #2 through #7. Once you've completed all 7 steps, let the fabrics age in their covered containers for at least 2 hours, or up to 24 hours.

Experiment!

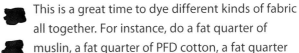
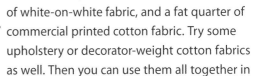
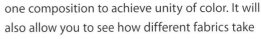

This is a great time to dye different kinds of fabric all together. For instance, do a fat quarter of muslin, a fat quarter of PFD cotton, a fat quarter of white-on-white fabric, and a fat quarter of commercial printed cotton fabric. Try some upholstery or decorator-weight cotton fabrics as well. Then you can use them all together in one composition to achieve unity of color. It will also allow you to see how different fabrics take the color differently. Be sure to prewash any commercial fabrics that you are going to overdye.

Dyeing Fabric Flat

In this chapter, I'll show you how to dye fabric flat instead of squishing it in a dishpan, as we did in the previous chapters. We'll use three different methods—using squirt bottles on fabric laid flat, stand-and-pour dyeing, and dye painting—to apply the dye. We'll use resists to create special looks and textures.

Basic equipment

You will need some large items such as a big, flat table and dye "platters" that you make out of Styrofoam and plastic (directions follow). You also need the following:

- Dyeing clothes and gloves, and a mask (if dyeing indoors)

- Clean plastic gloves for blending dyes

- 5-gallon plastic soaking bucket

- 12 plastic 1-cup squirt bottles from a dye supply house or beauty supplier

- Dye thickener, such as sodium alginate (see Resources, page 79)

- Paintbrushes in various sizes

- A large plastic container to set the platters in (especially if dyeing indoors)

- A clothesline or hangers for hanging the fabrics to dry (or you can spread them on the grass)

Setting up your workspace

So far we have dyed our fabrics squished in containers to achieve one mottled solid color. Now let's try some fun variations with the fabric laid flat.

You will need a place to lay out your fabric. I like to do my flat dyeing outdoors, where I can spread things out, use the garden hose, and generally not worry about making a mess. But you could also do flat dyeing in a basement, garage, or utility room.

I have a portable folding utility table made from molded plastic that is very lightweight. I set it up outdoors, but of course it would work indoors too. To make it a more comfortable height for me when I stand and dye, I use short lengths of PVC plastic pipe from a building supply store to extend the legs. The PVC pipe can be cut easily with an electric saw. (I use my husband's circular saw, but you can ask the salespeople to cut it for you at the store.) Just measure to figure out what length of pieces you need to bring the table up to the right height.

Fit PVC pipe on table legs to raise them.

Making dye platters

Of course, you are not going to dye right on the table surface. You will need a flat, portable surface to place the fabrics on while you dye them. I suggest that you make your own cheap, lightweight "dye platters." It's simple—all you need is Styrofoam insulation and a roll of plastic.

I buy Styrofoam insulation at a building supply store. It comes in 8′ × 4′ sheets and can easily be cut into three pieces. At the store, the salespeople usually will cut it for you on a big machine. Have the sheet cut in half so you have two pieces, each 4′ × 4′. Then ask the salesperson to cut one of those pieces in half again so you have two 4′ × 2′ pieces.

You will also need to buy a roll of plastic. I buy the kind designed for drop cloths. It is wide enough to wrap around the platters, and it's cheap. I cover the Styrofoam with this plastic using duct tape, which is more durable than masking tape. Wrap it up just like a package, and

tape it securely to fully enclose the Styrofoam. That way it is easy to rinse off, and you can use it over and over again.

Dyeing the fabric

Start with several yards of fabric cut into half-yard or full-yard pieces to fit on the dye platters. You can use plain white fabric. This is also a good time to try overdyeing commercial fabrics in a variety of ways. Just be sure to prewash commercial fabrics first.

To begin, prepare the fabric by presoaking it in sodium carbonate solution and spinning it in the washing machine (see Preparing the Fabric, page 12). Put one of the platters on top of the table and smooth out a piece of fabric on top of the platter.

You can dye with any or all of the gradations we did in the previous chapters of this book. I suggest you try one 12-step gradation at a time.

I mix up my dyes as described in Mixing the Basic Dyes (pages 12–14) and then make the gradations in each of the 12 squirt bottles.

I like to label all my squirt bottles with a permanent marker so I know what color is in each one. It is hard to tell the color just by looking at the bottle. I use numbers 1–12, but you can also put the name of the color—yellow-orange, for example—on the bottle if you like that better. Refer to the Gradation Chart in this book (page 15) or to a color wheel. (The labels will rub off over time, but just remark them.)

Then I begin to play.

Squirt bottles filled with mixed dyes

Reuse, recycle

Sodium carbonate water spinning out of washing machine into soaking bucket

If your washing machine drains into a utility sink, you can recycle and reuse the sodium carbonate solution. Put the wet fabric into the machine, and pour in the used soaking water with it. Put a 5-gallon bucket under the machine's drain hose in the utility sink. When you spin the fabric in the washing machine, the sodium water will drain back into the bucket, and you can use it again and again.

Method 1: Playing with squirt bottles

Take the squirt bottles with all the different dye colors and start applying color all over the fabric. Try different methods. On one half-yard piece, apply the colors in big circles. On another piece, apply the colors in big zig-zags. On a third piece, apply the colors in stripes from yellow all the way through to lime green. You get the idea. Just keep playing like this, trying different color combinations and different ways to apply the color.

Use your clean, gloved hands to blend the colors together. Remember, opposite colors on the color wheel will create brown, so keep that in mind when you place the colors next to each other. Brown can be good, but know what to expect and what colors you want to achieve when blending the colors. Your experience with dyeing the color wheel gradations in this book will help you know how colors blend.

Fabric on platter with blended dye colors

Adding resists

After you have applied the color, you can lay out the still-wet dyed fabric in the sun and place things on top of it to act as resists to create interesting patterns on the fabric. Try all kinds of objects. Anything that will lie flat and has some weight to it can be used as a resist. Rummage around the house to find stuff, and give it a try. Here is a list of things to start with:

- Rice, heavy grains, or dried peas
- Rock salt or Deka silk salt (see Resources, page 79)
- Rocks of all sizes
- Coins of all sizes
- Washers, nuts, and bolts from the hardware store
- Any flat or heavy found objects
- Scissors
- Pliers
- Glasses
- Bottles
- Marbles

To use rock salt or Deka silk salt, place it on top of the wet fabric, squirt it with water to get all the salt wet, and then let it dry. The salt will act as a resist and will send the color shooting out like stars.

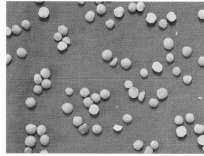

Peas acting as resist on wet fabric

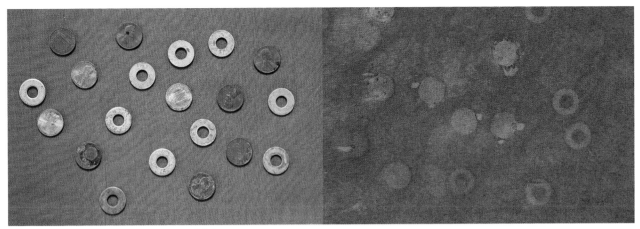

Coins and washers acting as resists on wet fabric

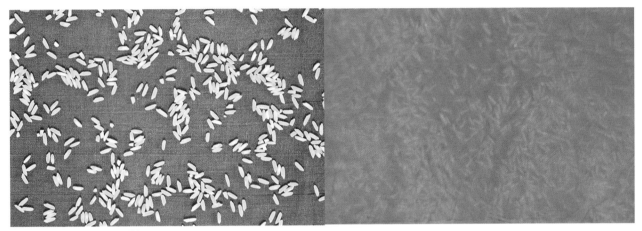

Rice acting as resist on wet fabric

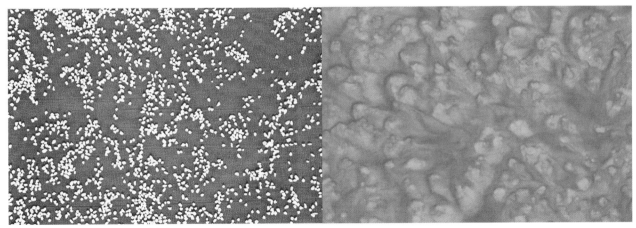

Rock salt acting as resist on wet fabric

Dry fabric with coin, rice, and salt resist designs

Method 2: Stand-and-pour dyeing

Another method to try on dye platters is the "stand and pour," or drip dyeing, method.

Place a length of presoaked and wrung-out fabric on the platter. Lean the platter up against a wall or table so that it stands at an 85° angle.

Dye platter ready for stand-and-pour dyeing

Starting at the top end of the fabric, use dye-filled squirt bottles to squirt dye on the fabric. The dye will drip and blend along the length of the fabric to the bottom. You will get some wonderful landscape and sky effects using this method.

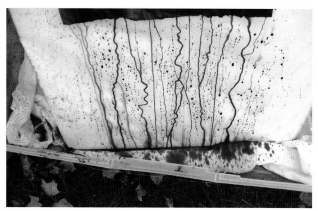

Excess dye runs to bottom to make mystery fabric.

Place the platter inside a large plastic container to catch the dripped dye. Place a piece of plain prepared fabric in the bottom of this container to catch the excess dye. Then you'll have yet another type of "mystery" fabric.

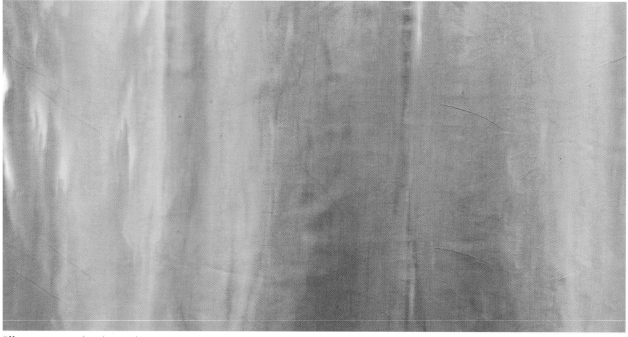

Effects using stand-and-pour dyeing

Method 3: Dye painting

Dye painting is closely related to stand-and-pour dyeing, but it is done with the platter lying flat. You can apply the dye with squirt bottles or with a paintbrush. With this method, use a thickener such as sodium alginate (derived from seaweed) to thicken the dye. Thickener is available from dye supply houses (see Resources, page 79). Follow the manufacturer's directions to mix it with your dyes.

You can create lots of interesting effects with the thickened dye. Squeeze it on using squirt bottles. Or use different types of paintbrushes to get different effects. A small brush will give you thin lines; you will get wide stripes with lines if you use a fat brush with bristles.

You can apply the thickened dye first, then let it dry and apply another unthickened color over it. Or, you can do just the opposite: dye the fabric first with unthickened dye, let it dry, and apply thickened dye over it. Either way will give interesting results. This is a great way to add texture to dyed fabric.

Effects created with thickened dye

Washing & Drying Your Fabric

WHEN FINISHING YOUR DYED FABRIC, KEEP IN MIND THESE HELPFUL TIPS:

- Make sure wet dyed fabrics don't sit touching each other.

- Wash and rinse your fabrics thoroughly.

- Iron the fabrics while damp for a crisp finish.

Now that you have dyed all this great colorful fabric, how do you wash it out and dry it so it's ready to use?

Aging the fabric

The dyed, wet fabrics need to sit and "age" for at least 2 hours, but ideally up to 24 hours. The amount of time required depends on the temperature, which should be at least 70°F (21°C). I have found that if I am working outside on a sunny day and the temperature is above 70°F, I can lay the fabrics out on the grass to dry. By the time they are dry, the color is set. Indoors, it takes longer.

Fabrics drying in sun

Washing out the fabric

When the sodium carbonate and dye have bonded and exhausted themselves, the excess dye can be washed away. The dye begins to lose its strength once it is mixed with the sodium carbonate, so you can't reuse any dye you squeeze out of your samples, even though the color still looks very intense.

I like to wash out light-colored fabrics by themselves instead of mixing them with darker-colored fabrics. However, if you stay right with the fabric and don't walk away from the washing machine between wash cycles, you can load them all together. You must remove and separate the fabrics immediately to make sure that none of them sit wet against each other. If they do, a transfer of unreacted dark dye against a lighter dye area will occur. This is called "backwash."

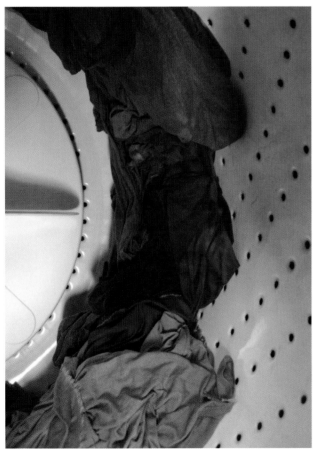

Backwashed fabric

I treat my dyed fabric the way I treated cloth diapers when my children were babies. I run them through a cold-water rinse cycle first, then a hot-water cycle with laundry detergent, and finally a double rinse cycle. By then, all the excess dye should be washed away.

Detergent 101

It doesn't matter what kind of detergent you use as long as it doesn't contain bleach.

Although I seldom use it, many people like to add Synthrapol to the wash cycle—use from 1 tablespoon to ¼ cup, depending on how much fabric you are washing. This product is a textile detergent used as a prewash for commercial fabrics. It is designed to keep dye in suspension when washing out fabrics, and it helps prevent backwash onto light-colored areas. You can buy Synthrapol through dye supply companies (see Resources, page 79) and sometimes in stores that sell dyes and fabric.

Final Rinse

In the final rinse, I add a little fabric softener. Make sure to follow the directions on the fabric softener bottle so that you don't get any spots on your newly dyed fabric. I usually put the fabric softener in a measuring cup and add water to it before I pour it into the wash water.

Drying and ironing your fabrics

I place the washed fabrics in the dryer to dry, but I like to take them out of the dryer still damp. They iron so much more beautifully when damp. And who doesn't like nice crisp, clean and lovely colored fabric to start playing with!

A good way to tell if all the excess dye is washed out of your fabrics is to iron them on a white cloth while still damp. If excess dye is lingering on the fabric, it will show up on the white cloth. If this happens, just put it through another wash and rinse cycle, and the dye should be all gone by then.

Cleaning up

How do you clean yourself, your clothes, and the laundry area after all this fun?

I usually throw my clothes, apron, and hand towels in the final wash with all my fabrics so that they are clean and good to go the next time I am ready to dye fabric.

I use one of the dirty hand towels to wipe down the washing machine around the rim, top, and sides before putting the cloth in the final wash. Once I take out the fabric, I also use a damp cloth to wipe off the inside of the washer where there might be some residual dye.

I wash and dry all my family's laundry in the same washer and dryer that I dye all my fabric in. The only time I have ever gotten any dye on my family's clothes was when I got careless in the dyeing process. Our clothes have never been affected by leftover dyes in the washing machine. The turquoise dye can leave a stain on the enamel of the washer or dryer, but it has never rubbed off on any laundry that I do.

There are products on the market to remove dye from your skin, but I have found that the best way to get rid of dye on my hands and arms—and in many instances, my legs and face—is to use a scrubby sponge and a nail brush. This method basically removes a layer of skin cells, so I think of it as going to a beauty spa. In the tub or sink, take the scrubby sponge to your body and pretend you are at an expensive spa resort where you are getting a mud scrub!

Sponge and nail brush

Gallery

Illinois Landscape, made and machine quilted by Frieda Anderson, 2009

Finished size: 42″ × 23″

I created this quilt from a sketch that I made while driving up to Wisconsin from Illinois. The farm fields and big sky are all that you see as you drive along the highway. This quilt was created using a free-form fused collage technique. The only quilting I did was stitching in-the-ditch to outline the shapes.

Finished size: 40″ × 48″

I always take pictures of flowers, trees, and landscapes when I travel. This quilt was inspired by a photo that I took of a bed of black-eyed Susans in front of an artisan shop in Virginia. I loved the way the flowers were all leaning to the left; they have a very Oriental feeling. I used silk charmeuse dyed in different shades of yellow to create the flowers in this quilt. The rest of the quilt is cotton. It is heavily machine quilted using rayon thread and a variegated cotton thread in the background. The binding is also raw-edge fused.

Summer Afternoon, made and machine quilted by Frieda Anderson, 2009

June Jubilee, made and machine quilted by Frieda Anderson, 2009

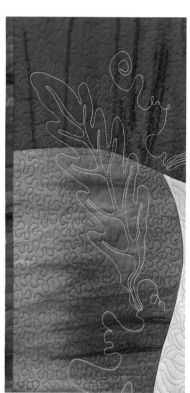

Detail of *June Jubilee*

Finished size: 60″ × 70″

This quilt was inspired by the poppies in my garden. Although mine are orange and melon-colored, I decided to make the poppies in this quilt magenta. Using silk charmeuse fabric, I dyed several different values of fuchsia for the flower heads because I knew how gorgeous they would look sitting on a complementary-colored background of lime green. The border fabric was pleated and dyed flat in shades of blue, turquoise, aqua, and green.

The poppy leaves in the border were stitched free-form in variegated cotton and stippled in several colors of rayon.

Spring's Greeting, made and machine quilted by Frieda Anderson, 2009

Detail of *Spring's Greeting*

Finished size: 38″ × 54″

I have a bed of daffodils planted by the west-facing windows of my house, and they bloom very early in the spring. Daffodils are such a wonderful treat after the long, hard Midwestern winters. I dyed many different shades of yellow silk for the flowers. For the wavy-edged background, I dyed silk flat in turquoise and painted on it with a sponge brush in lime green strokes for the leaves. The border fabric was pleated and dyed flat using lime green, green, aqua, and turquoise. I had a great time using silk thread to machine quilt large and small feather motifs.

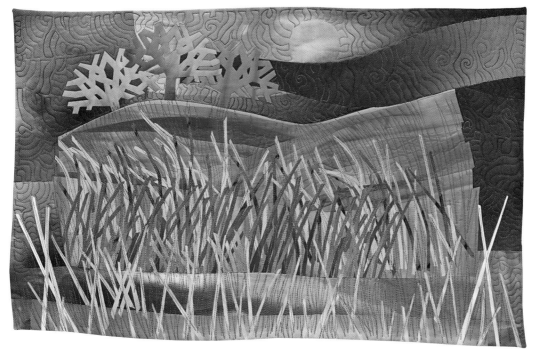

Beyond the Hill, made and machine quilted by Frieda Anderson, 2009

Finished size: 20″ × 29″

For this quilt I used a free-form fused collage technique to create the background, and then added the trees on the far horizon and the tall grass in the foreground. I used all twelve medium-value colors in the creation of this quilt.

Dancing Trees, made and machine quilted by Frieda Anderson, 2009

Finished size: 28″ × 32″

The trees in the woods where my dog and I walk are a great inspiration to me. From the first buds in the spring to the changing colors in the fall, they fascinate me. This quilt is a tribute to the hickory trees that are abundant in our woods. I love their elliptical shape and find that I am constantly using it in my quilts. This little quilt uses lots of contrasting colors in the leaves and sits on a background of blackened yellow. A border of fuchsia, red, and orange gives it a feeling of autumn. I used a decorative deckle blade to cut out the leaf shapes, and I free-motion machine quilted more leaves in the border with variegated cotton thread.

Sunset Pines, made and machine quilted by Frieda Anderson, 2009

Finished size: 20″ × 28″

Sunset Pines has dark- or blackened-value colors in the background and clear, bright oranges for the trees. These choices give depth and definition to the design. It is one of the few quilts that I have done as a vertical design. It has a pillowcase finish.

Midnight Forest, made and machine quilted by Frieda Anderson, 2009

Finished size: 34½″ × 27″

I constructed this quilt using a collage technique in much the same way that I did *Whispering Pines* (page 37). In this quilt, the color choices are just the reverse of those of *Whispering Pines*. The background behind the trees is silk charmeuse.

Gallery

Shimmering Foliage, made and machine quilted by Frieda Anderson, 2009

Finished size: 82″ × 82″

When I first started making quilts, I machine pieced all my designs. Over the years, I have done more and more fusing, but once or twice a year I still like to make a larger quilt that is pieced. *Shimmering Foliage* is pieced using orange made from warm Yellow #2 and red and lime greens made from both bright and warm yellows and blues. The border is all three values of fuchsia—light, medium, and dark. It is very densely quilted with stitching in-the-ditch around all the leaves and veins, and free-motion stick and twig designs in the background and border.

Whispering Pines, made and machine quilted by Frieda Anderson, 2009

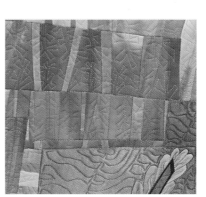

Detail of *Whispering Pines*

Finished size: 29″ × 36″

For this quilt I used a collage technique to create the background and borders. I chose colors that are opposites on the color wheel to make the quilt really pop. The background is silk charmeuse dyed flat; the borders and trees are all cotton. I free-motion quilted a pattern of sticks and twigs in the border and stipple quilted in the background behind the trees.

Georgie Porgie Puddin' and Pie, Pie for My Birthday, made and machine quilted by Frieda Anderson, 2009

Finished size: 24″ × 24″

This quilt, which features my dog George, is a raw-edge fused quilt. George himself is made from a light-to-dark gradation of turquoise on sateen fabric. The border was created by dyeing silk charmeuse flat, with all six colors mixed into the twelve gradations and then put in squirt bottles and applied to the wet fabric.

Dandelions, made and machine quilted by Frieda Anderson, 2009

Finished size: 48″ × 50″

Dandelions are ever-present in the Midwest where I live. I have often thought that they are the most beautiful yellow color, with a flower head that is so velvety and soft. I decided that they needed their own quilt. In the woods where I walk, they grow up out of last year's dead-oak-leaf carpet. That's why they are sitting on and surrounded by oak leaves in this quilt.

This was my first effort at making a completely fused raw-edge quilt design using my own hand-dyed fabrics. I outline stitched all the design elements and free-motion quilted the background and border.

Solar Flare II, made and machine quilted by Anne Lullie, 2009

Finished size: 20″ × 20″

"Like all the quilts in my Solar Flare series," says Ann, "this one is fusible appliqué, made with cotton and silk hand-dyed fabric. The shapes were cut freehand using fancy-edge rotary cutters. The circular and semicircular shapes were then arranged in a mandala design. The resulting quilt is vibrant and visually exciting and was lots of fun to make."

Pink Tulips, made and machine quilted by Emily Parson, 2009

Finished size: 40˝ × 50˝

Emily says, "Ten years ago, my husband and I left the city and bought our house in the Chicago suburbs. Because it was winter, we had no idea that beautiful daffodils and tulips were lying dormant in our yard, waiting to surprise us in the spring. That year, I became reacquainted with the joys of having a yard, flowers, birds, and wildlife. Since then, most of the quilts I have made have been my interpretation of the joy and beauty of nature. The unlimited colors of flowers, the patterns of butterflies, and the textures of leaves have not ceased to amaze and delight me. I hope to continue to draw on the vast and wonderful resource of nature, which has moved artists for centuries and continues to supply an unlimited palette of colors, textures, and ideas."

Gingko Sunrise, made and machine quilted by Ann Fahl, 2009

Finished size: 13½˝ × 9½˝

Photograph by Ann Fahl

"As a quilter," Ann says, "I love and protect my fabric collection. When I design and fabricate my large quilts, I always cut out extra leaves and flowers to practice my embroidery and quilting skills, and I save scraps fused with Wonder Under. Using this collection of tidbits, I created this playful quilt featuring a fountain-like center, which was formerly a good-sized brown triangle. This new shape is surrounded by colorful gingko leaves, wavy lines, and dots. The subjects are fused, machine embroidered, and hand beaded. The hand-dyed background fabric shades from green to orange, so I used green and orange rayon thread for the decorative quilting. The binding is made from commercial fabrics in orange print and a green stripe."

Housing Department #20, made and machine quilted by Laura Wasilowski, 2009

Finished size: 12˝ × 12˝

Laura says, "This is a whimsical view of my colorful neighborhood. The quilt is made with hand-dyed fabric and thread, fused, and finished with decorative hand stitches and machine quilting."

Fusing & Finishing Basics

I started quilting by making traditional pieced quilt tops. I love piecing, and I still do it. In fact, *Shimmering Foliage* (page 37) is an all-pieced quilt.

However, I have found that what I really like about fusing is that any idea I come up with can be translated into a quilt. Fusing allows me so much more freedom than traditional quilting methods, yet I still get to work with fabric. Fusing is also a logical choice because so many of the quilts that I design are intended to be viewed as artwork; they will hang on a wall and will never be washed or used like a traditional quilt. Fusing also allows me to be so much more organic with my designing.

In addition to fusing the designs on the quilt top, I fuse the quilt to the batting and fuse the binding. In this chapter, I have included basic instructions for fusing, along with directions for fused binding and pillowcase finishing. I hope these tips will help you have a successful fusing experience.

Easy fusing

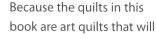
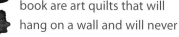
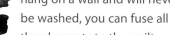
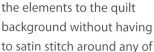

Because the quilts in this book are art quilts that will hang on a wall and will never be washed, you can fuse all the elements to the quilt background without having to satin stitch around any of the pieces.

Fusing basics

Follow these general instructions for making all the quilts in this book. Each project also includes any special instructions you need to make that particular quilt.

Fusing tools

- Rotary cutters with regular and decorative blades

- Small (18mm) rotary cutter (optional)

- Sharp embroidery scissors

- Rotary mat

- Ruler

- Black Sharpie extra-fine marker or mechanical pencil (I always use a mechanical pencil on lighter-colored fabrics.)

- Iron

- #805 Wonder Under fusible web

- Parchment paper (or use release paper from the fusible web)

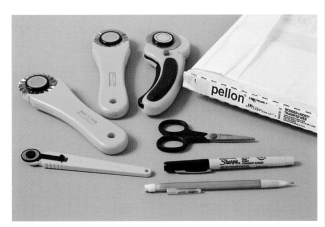

Fusing tools

Why I like Wonder Under fusible web

Paper-backed fusible web has dry glue on both sides; on one side is release (backing) paper. The heat of an iron activates the glue and transfers, or fuses, it to fabric. Then you can peel off the release paper and fuse the fabric to another piece of fabric.

I prefer 805 Wonder Under paper-backed fusible web (see Resources, page 79). Here's why:

- It is available at most fabric stores and is the least expensive.

- It is the widest product of its kind.

- It stays soft and supple.

- It works even if it peels off the paper (you can just press it back on).

- It rarely bleeds through the surface of most cottons and silks.

Also, the release paper is the best I've found for assembling fused fabrics.

Tip

  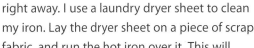 If you get fusible web on your iron, clean it off right away. I use a laundry dryer sheet to clean my iron. Lay the dryer sheet on a piece of scrap fabric, and run the hot iron over it. This will remove all the fusible web from the iron. Repeat as necessary. Clean the iron surface afterward on a separate piece of scrap fabric.

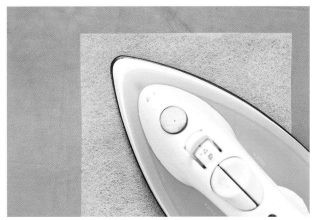

Press over dryer sheet on scrap fabric to clean iron.

Preparing fabric with fusible web

1. Before you begin, steam press the fabrics and batting to remove any wrinkles or creases. Then turn off the steam.

2. Cut the fusible web to fit inside the edges of the fabric so that the fusible web doesn't hang out beyond the fabric. This will help keep your ironing surface and iron clean.

3. Following the manufacturer's directions, use a hot, dry iron to apply fusible web to the back of each fabric you'll be using. (There is really no right or wrong side to hand-dyed fabrics.)

4. Let the fabric and fusible web cool, then peel away (and save) the release paper as you use each fabric.

Peel release paper off fabric.

Save that paper!

   Save all the release paper. You'll be using it throughout the process of fusing and constructing your quilt. But if you tear or ruin the release paper, you can use regular parchment paper from the grocery store instead.

Creating fused design elements

For some parts of your quilt designs, you will be tracing patterns onto fused fabric and cutting them out with scissors. For others—larger pieces as well as binding strips—you will use a rotary cutter.

I suggest that on your rotary cutting mat, you keep the fabric's fused side up. That way the fabric won't stick to the mat when you cut it.

Always try to cut out long, straight strips on the bias. That way you will be able to curve them easily, and it will also keep the edges from fraying.

Decorative rotary blades

 Decorative rotary blades come in many patterns—deckle, pinking, wave, scallop— that can add an extra design element to your quilts. When you are using a decorative rotary blade, turn your mat over to the wrong side, because the decorative blades can damage the mat.

 I like to have all my decorative blades in their own separate handles. That way I can switch back and forth without stopping to change the blades.

1. To transfer designs for the project elements from the pattern to the fused fabric, place a piece of release paper over the pattern. Using a Sharpie marker or mechanical pencil, trace around the outside shapes of the pattern sections for each fabric color.

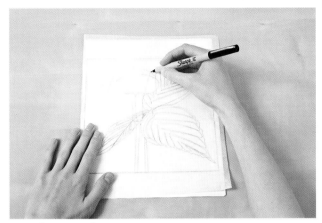

Trace design on release paper.

Note

Unlike other fusible appliqué methods, this technique requires the designs to be traced right side up onto the release paper. Also, any design elements that are adjacent to each other in the project will need to be overlapped, so make note of those areas when tracing them.

2. Place the release paper with the marked side against the fused side of the fabric. Press with a hot, dry iron to transfer the marked design to the back (fusible side) of the fused fabric. Remove the release paper.

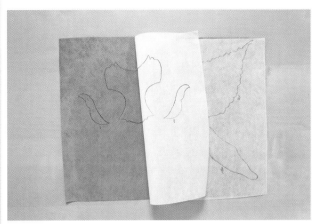

Design transferred to back of fused fabric

Release the release paper

 Cut out the shapes from the fused fabric without the release paper on it. That way you will get a clean, crisp edge that will not ravel and fray. Also, the paper can dull your scissors and rotary blades.

3. Use sharp embroidery scissors to cut out the shape. If it is a large shape, cut it out using a small (18mm) rotary cutter. Add a ¼″ allowance to areas that will extend under another piece.

Putting together fused design elements

Once you have fused and cut out all the elements of the design, you will place a clean piece of release paper over the pattern and arrange all the sections of the design in their proper positions. Sometimes I place them directly on the background fabric and just eyeball where to put them. You can do it either way—whatever feels most comfortable.

Designs for *Jack-in-the-Pulpit* (page 54) aligned over pattern on release paper

Because there are no seams in fused quilt tops, you will join the fabric pieces by overlapping them and fusing them together on the release paper. The pieces will need to overlap about ⅛″.

If you are joining a light colored piece to a darker colored piece, leave a ¼″ overlap on one side of the lighter piece. It is always best to put darker fabrics on top of lighter fabrics so there is no shadowing.

Darker fabric should overlap lighter fabric.

You will fuse-tack the fabric design elements before you do the final fusing onto the quilt top. Fuse-tacking means lightly ironing two pieces of fused fabric together, one slightly overlapping the other, on top of a piece of release paper. Press just enough to heat them so they stay together. You will be able to peel these as a unit from the release paper and trim the edges to get nice, clean lines. *Note:* If you are unsure how long to press, practice first on a test piece. You don't want to overheat at this point, because the fusible elements can get all fused up!

1. Once you have placed all the design elements in their proper places, carefully move the release paper, with the design elements on top, to an ironing surface, and fuse the design together on top of the release paper. (I suggest that you do not iron on top of the pattern, as the iron can cause the ink from the pattern to transfer to the back of the release paper.)

2. When the design has cooled, peel the whole thing up from the release paper, and place it on top of the background fabric.

3. Place a piece of clean release paper or parchment paper over the design, and fuse the design in place on the background fabric.

4. When the fabric is cool, peel it away from the release paper.

Layering and quilting

Now for the fun—putting it all together into a quilt top! Putting the quilt layers together couldn't be simpler. First, square up the quilt top using a rotary cutter and ruler. Place the finished quilt top on a piece of cotton batting, and fuse-tack it in place. Be very light-handed. You are just tacking the fabric lightly to the batting to adhere it—you are not pressing it on.

Finished *Jack-in-the-Pulpit* quilt top on top of batting

Batting and backing

 I like to use or Fairfield Natural Cotton or Hobbs Heirloom batting, which is a flat cotton batting.

 I use "mistake" fabric for my backings. For example, sometimes you dye fabric and it gets a spot on it, or maybe you really don't like the color. Simply use these fabrics for backings and sleeves.

Place this unit on top of the ironed backing fabric. Leave a little extra all around, and trim the batting and backing even with the quilt top.

Now you're ready to machine quilt your creation. If you plan to use the pillowcase finishing method (pages 47–48), you can wait and do the quilting last if you prefer.

I like to stitch in-the-ditch around all the design elements of my quilts. For straight edges, I start out with the machine feed dogs up, using a regular straight stitch. To stitch around the design elements, I put the feed dogs down and use an embroidery foot. Using a thread color that matches whatever design element I am stitching around, I free-motion stitch around all the elements, stitching right next to (not on top of) the design element.

Colorful thread

 I like to use rayon thread for machine quilting. I especially like the huge selection of colors that is available.

Finishing your quilts

I have included two methods for finishing the edges of quilts—the fused binding method and the pillowcase method. Both are easy—the choice is up to you! Just keep in mind that with a fused binding, you will want to do the quilting before you bind, as for any other quilt.

Making a fused binding

Basic tools

- Rotary cutter with regular blade
- Decorative rotary blades, such as deckle, pinking, wave, or scallop—your preference*
- Rotary cutting mat
- Ruler
- Colored pencils

* I keep several rotary cutters, each with a different decorative blade on it.

Directions for binding

> **Note**
>
> If you are putting a sleeve on the quilt, make the sleeve (pages 48–49) and sew the unfinished edge of the sleeve along the top edge on the back of the quilt after you have squared it up. Then continue to add the binding.

1. Fuse web to the back of the binding fabric as described on page 42.

2. Allow the fabric to cool, then peel off and save the release paper.

3. You will cut 4 lengths of fabric, each about 1½″ to 2″ longer than needed for the edges of the quilt. Use a rotary cutter with a regular blade to cut the first edge of a strip, then move your ruler over 1¼″, and use a decorative blade to cut the other edge. Continue alternating the cutters to cut all 4 strips, each with one straight edge and one decorative edge. The binding will be folded in half, with the decorative edge on top of the quilt.

Binding strips with one straight and one decorative edge

4. Square up the layered quilt top, and mark ½″ in from each edge with a colored pencil that roughly matches the quilt color.

Quilt top marked ½″ from inside edges

5. Bind the top and bottom edges first. Lay the quilt face up on your ironing surface, with a piece of release paper under the side edge that you will bind first. Place the decorative edge of a binding strip on top of the quilt, slightly overlapping the colored pencil line. Half the binding's width will extend beyond the edge of the quilt to rest on the release paper.

6. Using a hot, dry iron, press the binding in place. Let this cool, and then peel the extending half of the binding off the release paper.

7. Flip the quilt over, and fold the other half of the binding to the back. Fuse it in place.

8. Turn the quilt face up again, and repeat Steps 5 through 7 on the opposite edge of the quilt. Trim the binding ends flush with the quilt side edges.

Two sides of quilt with fused binding

9. Bind the quilt side edges with pieces of binding that are at least 1″ longer than the quilt top's height.

10. With the quilt face up on a piece of release paper, position the binding strips on the side edges in the same way you did for the top and bottom strips, and fuse into place.

11. Let the fabric cool, and peel the extending halves of the binding off the release paper. On the back of the quilt, tuck the ends around to the back at the corners, and fold them in.

Quilt back with binding folded over before fusing

12. Place a piece of fusible web on top of each tucked-in corner, and then fold the rest of the binding to the back; and fuse in place with a hot, dry iron.

13. Topstitch the binding on the front of the quilt, using decorative thread if you wish.

Making a pillowcase finish

Begin with the squared-up quilt top and batting unit, and trim the backing fabric to the exact size as the quilt top. You can cut the edges curvy instead of straight if the project calls for it.

1. Trim off an extra ⅛″ from the top and left side of the backing to make it slightly smaller than the quilt top.

2. On the wrong side of the backing fabric, an inch or so below the top edge, place a piece of fusible web that is 1″ shorter than the width of the quilt top and 2″–3″ wide. Fuse this in place, and cut a slit through the middle of it along its length. Leave the release paper on the fusible web for now.

3. Place the backing fabric and the quilt "sandwich" right sides together, slightly stretching the backing fabric to fit the front, and pin it at all 4 corners.

Backing with fusible strip, pinned to front sandwich

4. Machine stitch around the outside edge using a ¼″ seam allowance.

5. Trim the corners as shown.

Trim bulk from corners.

6. Press all the seams open before turning the whole unit right side out.

Press seams flat.

7. Turn the quilt right side out through the slit that you cut through the fusible web on the backing fabric.

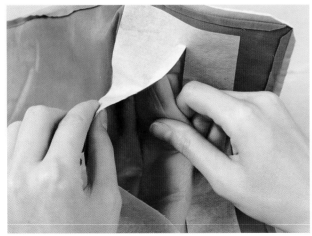

Turn quilt inside out through slit in back.

8. Finger-press all 4 sides, rolling the seams to the back side of the quilt. Use a point turner in the corners if necessary.

9. Once you have pressed all the seams and rolled them to the back, pull the paper off the fusible web inside. Fuse the slit in the back of the quilt closed.

10. Machine quilt your creation.

Making a pleated quilt sleeve

It is just as important to have a neat and carefully crafted sleeve on your treasured quilt as it is to have a neat and carefully crafted quilt.

Making a pleat in the quilt sleeve will allow the quilt to hang on the wall much flatter and is well worth the trouble of creating it. Even on my small quilts, I always put a 4″ sleeve on the back with a ½″ pleat in it, so that a rod in the sleeve will not cause a bulge at the top of the quilt.

Following are directions for a sleeve with a ½″ pleat.

1. Measure the width of the finished, squared-up quilt before binding. Cut a 10″-wide piece of fabric at least ¾″ to 1″ longer than the width of the finished quilt.

2. Fold over ½″ on each short end, and press. Fold over another ½″, and press. Stitch the folded edges down with a straight stitch to neatly finish off the sleeve ends.

3. Fold the sleeve in half lengthwise, right sides out, to create an open-ended tube 5″ wide and 1″ shorter than the width of the quilt. Press.

4. With the tube still on your ironing surface, bring the front half of the sleeve up ⅜″ over the top of the back side, and press. This creates a second crease that will be on the back side of the sleeve when it is folded back to the first crease and even at the top. You can open up the sleeve and stitch a straight line along this fold to use as a guide later when you fold it up to stitch it to the back of the quilt.

Fold up ⅜″.

5. Open up the sleeve, and machine stitch the quilt label to the center of the sleeve on the front side.

6. Fold the top flap back down to the first crease mark, with the 2 edges flush at the top. Pin along the top length, and stitch the top together along the long side using a ¼″ seam.

7. On the top edge of the quilt, find the center, and center the sleeve along this edge with the raw edges at the top meeting flush. Using a ¼″ seam allowance, sew the sleeve in place. Now sew on the binding all around the quilt.

For the pillowcase finish, create the sleeve in the same manner, only fold the sleeve right sides together, sew the top opening closed, and turn it inside out. Pin the sleeve along the top of the quilt.

8. Hand stitch the sleeve in place. To create the pleat, push the sleeve unit up so that the second pressed crease with the stitched guideline that was on the back of the sleeve is the crease that you hand stitch in place. Once it is sewn in place, you can press the sleeve again to create a crease at the top by the quilt binding.

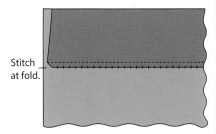

Stitch at fold.

Hand stitch bottom of sleeve in place.

Making a label

I like to make my labels by running fabric with Wonder Under on it through my inkjet printer.

I fuse the fabric and leave the paper on, and I trim the fabric to 8½″ × 11″. Then I run it through the inkjet printer, printing all the information on the label. I cut out the label using a decorative blade in my rotary cutter. Then I fuse the label to the quilt sleeve and sew around the label before I put the sleeve on the quilt. I usually sign the label as well, with a Sharpie marker. I think it is very important that we document the things we make.

Label and sleeve on back of quilt

Once I am completely finished with the quilt, I give it a good steam pressing with a pressing cloth covering the surface.

Jack-in-the-Pulpit

FINISHED SIZE: 12″ × 14″

Made and machine quilted by Frieda Anderson

Many of my quilts start out as drawings. I love to walk in the woods near my home with my dog, George, and much of my inspiration for artwork comes from these daily walks. Jack-in-the-pulpits are one of my favorite early summer plants that grow in our little woods. I sat on the woodland floor to draw a picture, which then became this quilt.

I made this quilt using silk charmeuse fabric that I dyed exactly the same way I dye cotton fabric. I love using silk to fuse quilt tops, because it gives the quilts such luminosity. But you could certainly use cottons as an alternative.

My jack-in-the-pulpit drawing

Materials

All fabrics are dyed with Dharma Trading dyes. Unless otherwise indicated, all colors are medium value. If you are dyeing fabrics for this project, dye fat quarters of the colors listed. The amounts of fabric given below are the minimum amounts needed to make this quilt.

Scrap at least 8″ × 9″ of green fabric (Bright Gradation Step 11) for Sections 1–5

Scrap at least 4″ × 7½″ of green fabric (Warm Gradation Step 11) for Sections 6–9

Scrap at least 7½″ × 8½″ of lime green fabric (Warm Gradation Step 12) for Sections 10–13

Fat quarter of lime green fabric (Bright Gradation Step 12) for background and Section 14

Fat quarter of green fabric (Warm Gradation Step 11) for border

14″ × 16″ piece of fabric for backing

14″ × 16″ piece of flat cotton batting

1½ yards of fusible web

Hand-dyed fabrics for *Jack-in-the-Pulpit*

Preparing the fabrics

Apply fusible web to the backs of all the fabrics, as described in Fusing Basics, pages 41–42.

Let the fabric and fusible web cool. As you use each piece of fabric, remove and save the release paper.

Making the background and border

1. Place the border fabric on a cutting mat with the fusible side up, and cut out a piece 13″ × 15″. Place it fusible side down on a piece of release paper that is larger than the fabric.

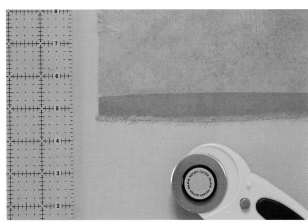
Cut backing fabric fused side up on cutting mat.

2. Place the background fabric fusible side up on the cutting mat, and cut out a piece 8″ × 9¼″. Place it fusible side down on another piece of release paper.

Making the jack-in-the-pulpit, leaves, and stems

Refer to Creating Fused Design Elements and Putting Together Fused Design Elements on pages 42–44.

Now you will cut and assemble all the parts of the design. Just in case you're tempted to fuse the design pieces to the background as you go—don't! You will put the whole thing together and then fuse it to the background.

1. Peel the release paper off the first green fabric (Bright Gradation Step 11). Place the release paper over the pattern (Step 1, page 43), and with a Sharpie marker or a mechanical pencil, trace around Sections 1–5.

2. Transfer the marked pattern from the release paper to the fabric's fused side as shown on Step 2, page 43 using a hot, dry iron. Remove the release paper.

3. Use sharp embroidery scissors to cut out the design elements. See page 43 for tips on cutting and placing overlapped design elements. Place them on a separate piece of release paper.

4. Repeat Steps 1–3, tracing and transferring Sections 6–9 to the fused side of the green fabric (Warm Gradation Step 11).

5. Repeat the same steps, tracing and transferring Sections 10–13 to the fused side of the lime green fabric (Warm Gradation Step 12).

6. Repeat the same steps, tracing and transferring Section 14 to the fused side of the lime green fabric (Bright Gradation Step 12).

7. Place a clean piece of release paper or parchment paper over the pattern, and line up all the design elements in their proper places on the paper. Carefully move the release paper, with the design elements on top, to an ironing surface, and fuse the design together on top of the release paper.

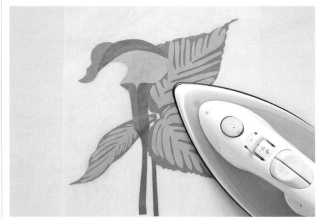
Fuse design on top of release paper.

Putting together the quilt top

1. Peel the cooled design off the release paper, and place it on the prepared background. Trim the jack-in-the-pulpit stems even with the bottom of the background.

2. Place a piece of clean parchment paper over the design, and fuse it in place on the background.

3. Peel off the paper, and use a ruler and rotary cutter to square up the background piece.

4. Place the trimmed background piece slightly off-center on the border fabric, and fuse it in place.

Finishing the quilt

Refer to Making a Pillowcase Finish (pages 47–48) to finish this quilt. Then follow up with the machine quilting.

For this quilt, I stitched in-the-ditch around the darker green design elements using turquoise thread, and around the lighter green elements using green thread. Next, I stipple quilted the background using a matching lime green 60-weight thread.

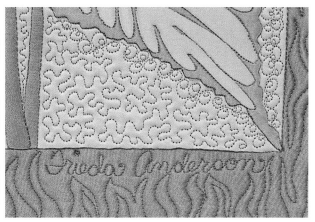
I quilted my name in the border.

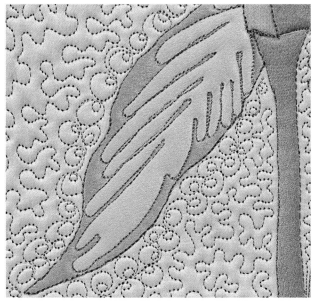
In-the-ditch quilting and stippling

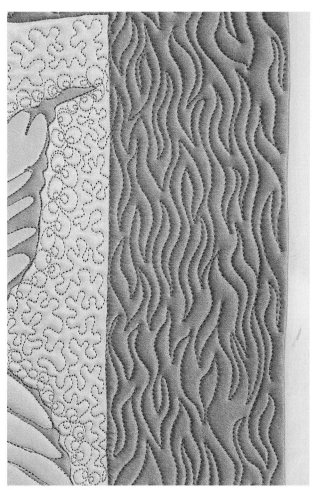
Free-motion quilting in border

I machine quilted my name in the border of the quilt and then, in the rest of the border, stitched a free-motion design that reminds me of bark.

Finally, I hand stitched a sleeve on the back of the quilt to cover up the slit in the back where I turned the quilt inside out. Refer to Making a Pleated Quilt Sleeve on pages 48–49.

Jack-in-the-Pulpit pattern

Irises

Made and machine quilted by Frieda Anderson

As flowers begin to bloom in the spring and summer, I take my lawn chair, sketchbook, and pencils out in my garden in the early morning. My dog, George, sits with me while I sketch the different flowers as they bloom throughout the season. Irises are some of my favorites; I love the contrast of colors between the stamen and the petals. I hope you will enjoy making this sweet quilt.

My iris drawing

Materials

All fabrics are dyed with Dharma Trading dyes. Unless otherwise indicated, all colors are medium value. If you are dyeing fabrics for this project, dye fat quarters of the colors listed. The amounts of fabric given below are the minimum amounts needed to make this quilt.

Scrap at least 11″ × 10″ of violet fabric (Warm Gradation Step 7) for flowers and buds

Scrap at least 4″ × 7″ of yellow-orange fabric (Warm Gradation Step 2) for iris stamens

Scrap at least 3″ × 4″ of orange fabric (Bright Gradation Step 3) for iris sepals

Scraps at least 13″ × 11″ each of green (Warm Gradation Step 11) and blue-green (Warm Gradation Step 10) fabric

Fat quarter of blue-violet fabric (Bright Dark-Value Gradation Step 8) for border

Fat quarter of fabric for binding

17″ × 20″ piece of fabric for backing

17″ × 20″ piece of flat cotton batting

2⅝ yards of fusible web

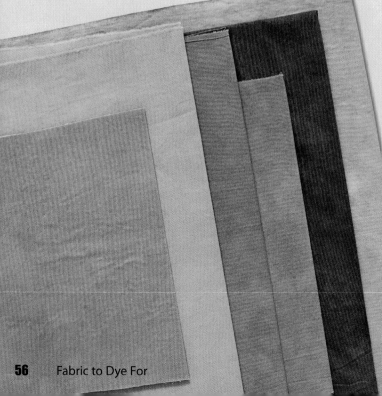

Hand-dyed fabrics for Irises

Preparing the fabrics

Apply fusible web to the backs of all the fabrics, as described in Fusing Basics, pages 41–42.

Let the fabric and fusible web cool. As you use each piece of fabric, remove and save the release paper.

Layer the batting with the backing fabric, pressing them together to get a nice, smooth sandwich. Set this aside.

Making the background and border

1. Remove the release paper from the border and background fabrics.

2. Place the border fabric on a cutting mat with the fusible side up. Cut a piece 16½″ × 20½″, which will be about ½″ larger than the finished quilt size. Place this piece back on the release paper.

3. Place the background fabric fused side up on your rotary mat, and cut out a rectangle 9¾″ × 11¼″. Place this piece back on the release paper. You will build the iris design on top of this.

Making the iris stems and leaves

1. Peel off the release paper from the green and blue-green fabrics.

2. To make the leaves, place the fabrics fused side up on your rotary mat. Using a ruler and rotary cutter, cut 4 strips on the bias, ¾″ × 12″ from each fabric. Cut 3 strips on the bias, ½″ × 7″ from blue-green fabric and 6 strips ½″ × 7″ from green fabric.

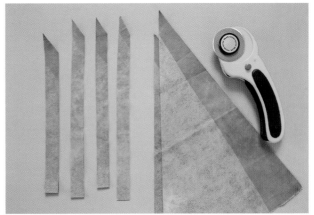

Cut out leaves on bias.

3. Using a rotary cutter, taper one end of each leaf to a point.

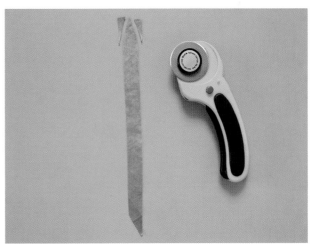

Taper end of each leaf.

4. Enlarge the iris pattern (page 60) to 125%. Place a piece of release paper over the enlarged pattern, and position each leaf piece over the picture and on top of the release paper. Or you can do what I do—I just eyeball the placement on the background fabric. Once you like the arrangement, fuse-tack the leaves in place. You may want to trim the leaves that extend beyond the background fabric at this point, or you can wait until later. *Note:* I chose to have one of the stems and a flower petal go behind a leaf. Careful fuse tacking will allow you to make these minor changes as you go.

Leaves on background fabric

5. Using a ruler and rotary cutter, cut out 4 stems on the bias, each about ¼″–⅜″ × 9″, from the green fabric. Place these in position on the release paper, or place on the background fabric. Do not fuse-tack these yet.

Making the flowers and buds

Now you will cut and assemble the design pieces for the irises.

1. Remove the release paper from the violet fabric. Place the release paper on the enlarged iris pattern, and trace around the elements for the iris flowers and bud heads as described on pages 42–43.

2. Using sharp embroidery scissors, cut out the flower and bud shapes.

3. Place each flower and bud over its outline on the picture on the release paper, lining up the stem underneath it. (Or, again, simply eyeball the placement on the fabric.) Once you like the placement, fuse-tack the stems in place.

4. Place a piece of release paper over the pattern, and trace around the sepal, which is the part right under the flower. You can make this out of darker green or brown. I have made mine from a scrap of orange. Transfer this to a piece of fused fabric, and cut it out. Place it under the flower, and fuse-tack the sepals and flowers in place.

5. Place a piece of release paper over the pattern, and trace around the stamen of the iris using a mechanical pencil. Transfer this to the back of the yellow-orange fabric. Using sharp embroidery scissors, cut out the stamens, and place them on the irises. Fuse-tack in place.

Putting together the quilt top

1. Remove the whole design from the release paper, and place it on top of the background fabric. (If you used the "eyeball" placement method, you have already placed the elements on the background.) Fuse it all in place.

2. Remove the release paper from the back of the background fabric, and, using a rotary cutter and ruler, trim this background piece to 9½″ × 11″.

3. Place the fused background unit on the border fabric. I have positioned mine off-center—approximately 2½″ from the top and 5″ from the bottom, and with an equal 3″ space on each side. Refer to the quilt photo on page 55.

4. Place the whole unit on top of the pressed backing unit, and fuse-tack in place. Pin at the 4 corners.

Machine quilting the quilt

I always like to stitch in-the-ditch on all straight edges, so I started out with the feed dogs up and used a straight regular stitch around the background fabric. I used a darker thread, but you can use whatever suits your fancy.

Then I stitched in-the-ditch around all the leaves and stems, using a darker green thread and a straight stitch. Next, I switched to a free-motion stitch, dropped my feed dogs, and outline stitched around the irises and buds using violet thread. Then I switched to orange thread and did the same around the stamen. Finally, I switched to brown thread and outline stitched around the sepal.

I decided to extend the design outside the background into the border by repeating the iris shape.

First, I traced around the shape of the iris on a piece of release paper. Then I cut out the shape from the release paper and, with a chalk pencil, drew the design in the border area. Next, I free-motion quilted the iris shape with violet thread.

Outline stitching

I extended the design of the leaves into the bottom border, using green straight stitching.

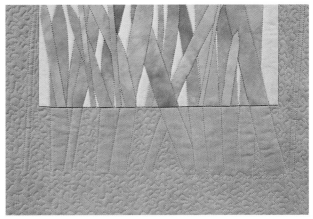
Stitching extended into border

Finally, I stipple quilted the whole border area with matching thread. I also free-motion quilted my name in the border area.

To finish your quilt, refer to Making a Fused Binding (pages 46–47) and Making a Pleated Quilt Sleeve (pages 48–49). Add a label, as described on page 49, if you wish.

Iris pattern; Enlarge 125% before tracing.

Daily Walk

Made and machine quilted by Frieda Anderson

Every day I walk with my dog, George, along a path in a little 22-acre wood near my home. George runs around smelling and chasing things while I enjoy the scenery. We both miss it if we don't get there, so we go rain or shine. This quilt is a portrait of George, looking at me and telling me he is not ready to go home yet.

This quilt shows how fun it can be to mix and match dyed fabrics. I have used two different color gradations and several overdyed fabrics in this project. Remember, you don't always have to make things look realistic. Have fun, and be fanciful and experimental with your color choices.

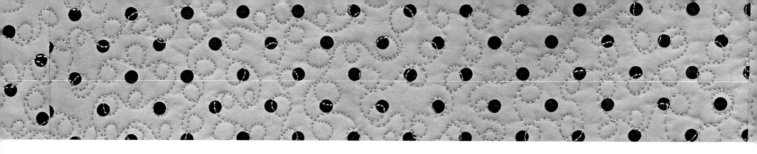

Materials

All fabrics are dyed with Dharma Trading dyes. Unless otherwise indicated, all colors are medium value. If you are dyeing fabrics for this project, dye fat quarters of the colors listed. The amounts of fabric given below are the minimum amounts needed to make this quilt.

For George:

Scrap at least 8″ × 9″ of violet fabric (Bright Gradation Step 7)

Scrap at least 8″ × 9″ of blue-violet fabric (Warm Gradation Step 8)

Scrap at least 3″ × 3″ of blue fabric (Warm Light-Value Gradation Step 9)

Scrap at least 3″ × 4″ of blue-violet fabric (Warm Gradation Step 8) for George's collar

Scrap at least 2″ × 2″ of yellow-orange fabric (Bright Dark-Value Gradation Step 2) for George's tag

For the background sections:

Scrap at least 5″ × 14″ of yellow-green (Warm Gradation Step 12) overdyed print fabric for foreground (Section 1)

Scrap at least 5″ × 14″ of yellow-green fabric (Bright Dark-Value Gradation Step 12) for background (Section 2)

Scrap at least 10″ × 14″ of blue fabric (Bright Light-Value Gradation Step 9) for sky (Section 3)

Scrap at least 3½″ × 14″ of blue fabric (Bright Gradation Step 9) for cloud (Section 4)

Scrap at least 7″ × 10″ of yellow-orange fabric (Warm Gradation Step 2) for trees

Scrap at least 6″ × 6″ of red-orange fabric (Bright Dark-Value Gradation Step 4) for path

For the border:

Fat quarter of green (Bright Dark-Value Gradation Step 11) overdyed black-on-white dot fabric

Fat quarter of fabric for binding

22″ × 22″ piece of fabric for backing

22″ × 22″ piece of flat cotton batting

3½ yards of fusible web

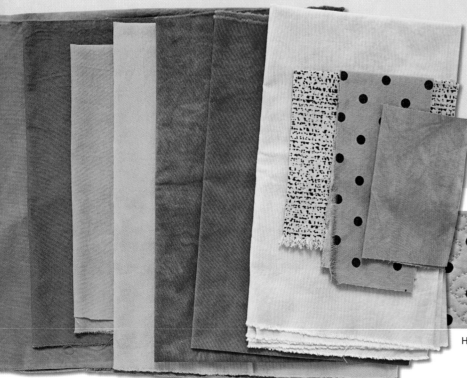

Hand-dyed fabrics used in Daily Walk

Preparing the fabrics

Apply fusible web to the backs of all the fabrics, as described in Fusing Basics, pages 41–42.

Let the fabric and fusible web cool. As you use each piece of fabric, remove and save the release paper.

Layer the batting with the backing fabric, pressing them together to get a nice, smooth sandwich. Set this aside.

Making George

1. Enlarge the *Daily Walk* pattern (page 65) to 185%. Follow the directions in Creating Fused Design Elements (page 42–43) to transfer all the design elements for George and for his collar and tag from the enlarged pattern to the backs of the fused fabrics.

2. Assemble George on top of a piece of release paper, and fuse-tack him together. Next, fuse-tack his collar, trimming it if necessary on the sides after you have fused it in place. Fuse-tack the tag. Set George aside while you create the background.

George, assembled on release paper

Dog tag tip

Before I cut out the shape for George's tag, I typed his name in my computer and ran the tag fabric through my inkjet printer. You could also print a name on the tag using a permanent marker.

Making the background

1. Transfer the design for Section 1 onto the yellow-green overdyed fabric. Cut it out exactly on the lines.

2. Transfer the design for Section 2 onto the lime green fabric. When you cut out this section, leave a scant ¼″ extra on the bottom section so that you can lap Section 1 over Section 2 on a piece of release paper. Fuse-tack these together.

3. Transfer the design for Section 3 onto the back of the light blue sky fabric. Cut this out, leaving a scant ¼″ extra on the bottom edge so that you can lap Section 2 over Section 3. Do not fuse-tack yet.

4. Transfer the design for Section 4 onto the back of the blue cloud fabric, and cut it out exactly on the lines. Lay this on top of Section 3.

5. Transfer the design for the trees onto the back of the yellow-orange fabric. Cut them out, leaving extra on the top and bottom for overlap. Lay the trees on the light blue sky background, tucking the trunks under Section 2 and the limbs under Section 4. Fuse-tack the whole background together.

Trees transferred to fused fabric

6. Peel up George from the release paper, and place him on the background.

7. Transfer the design for the path onto the back of the red-orange fabric. Cut this out exactly on the lines. Place it on the green part of the background, and fuse-tack in place.

8. From the border fabric, cut out strips that are 3½″ wide × 20″ long.

9. Square up the background piece to 13″ × 13″. Place a strip of border fabric over the top and bottom, slightly overlapping the background square. Fuse-tack the pieces together on a piece of release paper. Trim the ends of the borders even with the background sides, and add the side borders, again slightly overlapping the background as well as the ends of the top and bottom borders.

Border being built up around background

10. Peel this off the release paper, and place it on the pressed batting/backing sandwich. Fuse-tack the top to the batting.

11. Pin at the 4 corners.

Machine quilting the quilt

I started quilting *Daily Walk* by outline stitching Sections 2, 3, and 4 with the feed dogs up and using a straight stitch. Then I outline stitched around the trees and path. Next, I switched to a free-motion foot, dropped my feed dogs, and outline stitched around all the elements of George. Finally, I switched back to a straight stitch and outline stitched around the whole background. Once all the outline stitching was done, I went back and did filler stitching, such as the stippling and circles in the sky and the squiggles in the grass area. The last thing I did was the free-motion quilting in the border.

To finish, I squared up the quilt. Mine measured 20″ × 20″, but yours could be different.

Refer to Making a Fused Binding (pages 46–47) and Making a Pleated Quilt Sleeve (pages 48–49) to finish off the quilt. Add a label, as described on page 49, if you wish.

Section 4

Section 3

Section 2

George

Section 1

Daily Walk pattern; Enlarge 185% before tracing.

Made and machine quilted by Frieda Anderson

I love living in the Midwest because the landscape is very soothing to me, and driving through the countryside seems to ground me. The idea for this quilt came to me on one of those drives along the highway—it was in Wisconsin or Iowa—in the autumn. As you drive along, you pass rolling hills with rows of trees along each horizon. The trees seem to act as dividers in the landscape.

When you work on this project, you'll be using decorative rotary blades a lot. Check the helpful tips in Decorative Rotary Blades, page 42.

Materials

All fabrics are dyed with Dharma Trading dyes. Unless otherwise indicated, all colors are from the Warm Color dark-value gradation. If you are dyeing fabrics specifically for this project, dye fat quarters of the colors listed. (Borders and backing will require larger amounts.) The amounts of fabric given below are the minimum amounts needed to make this quilt.

For background Sections 1–5 and trees:

Fat quarter of blue-green fabric (Step 10)

Fat quarter of green fabric (Step 11)

Fat quarter of lime or yellow-green fabric (Step 12)

Fat quarter of blue-violet fabric (Step 8)

Fat quarter of blue fabric (Step 9)

For the trees:

Piece at least 4″ × 7″ of yellow-orange fabric (Step 2)

Piece at least 5″ × 18″ of orange fabric (Step 3)

Piece at least 5″ × 18″ of red-orange fabric (Step 4)

Piece at least 5″ × 18″ of red-violet fabric (Step 6)

Piece at least 10″ × 18″ of violet fabric (Step 7)

For the tree trunks:

Piece at least 14″ × 14″ of red fabric (Step 5)

½ yard of yellow fabric (Step 1) for border

Fat quarter of fabric for binding

25″ × 28″ piece of fabric for backing

25″ × 28″ piece of flat cotton batting

4½ yards of fusible web

Note: You will also need a sheet of craft paper or newsprint at least 18″ × 15″.

Hand-dyed fabrics used in *Autumnal Trees*

Preparing the fabrics

1. Apply fusible web to the backs of all the fabrics, as described in Fusing Basics (pages 41–42).

2. Let the fabric and fusible web cool. As you use each piece of fabric, remove and save the release paper.

3. Layer the batting with the backing fabric, pressing them together to get a nice, smooth sandwich. Set this aside.

Creating the background pattern

1. On a sheet of craft paper or newsprint, draw a rectangle 18″ × 15″. This is the center of the center panel for *Autumnal Trees*.

2. On the right side of the rectangle, measure up 6″ from the bottom corner, and make a mark. Then measure along the bottom 6″ to the left of the corner, and make a mark. Draw a curved line between the 2 marks to create Section 1.

3. On the left side of the rectangle, measure up 1″ from the bottom corner, and make a mark. Draw a curved line from this mark to the 6″ mark on the right side of the rectangle. This creates Section 2.

4. On the left side of the rectangle, measure up 7″ from the first 1″ mark (8″ total), and make a mark. On the right side, measure up 7″ from the first 6″ mark (13″ total), and make a mark. Draw a curved line between these 2 marks. Along

this curved line, measure 10″ over from the right side, and make a mark. Draw a curved line from this mark down to the first 6″ mark on the right side of the rectangle. This creates Sections 3 and 4. Section 5 is the top area that is left.

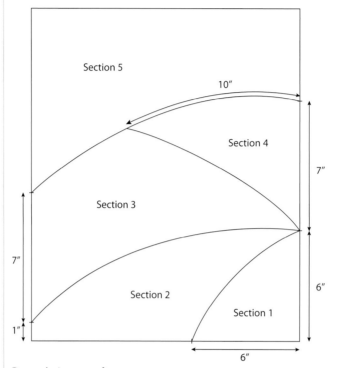

Drawn design on craft paper

Making the background hills and the treetops

Use the following fabrics for each section. Or, if you prefer, feel free to make your own choices.*

Section Number	Background Fabric	Tree Top Fabric
Section 1	Blue–violet (Step #8)	Yellow–orange (Step #2), orange (Step #3)
Section 2	Blue (Step #9)	Orange (Step #3), red–orange (Step #4)
Section 3	Blue–green (Step #10)	Red–orange (Step #4), violet (Step #7)
Section 4	Green (Step #11)	Red–violet (Step #6), violet (Step #7)
Section 5	Yellow–green (Step #12)	Red–violet (Step #6), blue–violet (Step #8)

*The tree trunks are all made of one fabric: Red (Step #5).

1. Remove the release paper from the blue background fabric, and place it on top of the craft-paper pattern you just created. With a black Sharpie marker, trace around Section 1. Place the release paper marker side down on the fused side of the fabric, and press with a hot, dry iron to transfer the shape.

2. With the fused side of the fabric facing up on your rotary mat, cut out the shape, adding a ¼″ seam allowance on the outside straight edges but not on the top curve. For all the other sections, you will add a ¼″ seam allowance on the bottom curved edge only. This is so you can slightly overlap, or "seam", each section.

Place Section 1 on another piece of release paper and set aside.

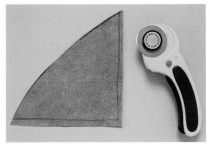

Cut out Section 1.

3. On the release paper pattern for Section 1, draw 3 elliptical tree shapes in graduated sizes to fill the space from side to side. Refer to the tree placement diagram and the quilt photo (page 66) for the shapes, or, if you don't want to draw the trees, enlarge the diagram to 350% and trace the shapes.

Tree placement diagram

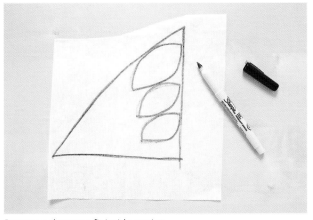

Draw tree shapes to fit inside section.

4. Remove the release paper from the yellow-orange and orange treetop fabrics. Place the Section 1 pattern on the fused side of the orange fabric, and press with a hot, dry iron to transfer the tree shapes. Layer the orange fabric on top of the yellow-orange fabric, fused sides up. With a deckle blade in your rotary cutter, cut out the tree shapes slightly outside the lines and through both layers of fabric.

Marked tree fabric layered on top of unmarked tree fabric

5. Switch to a regular-blade rotary cutter, and cut each tree shape in half from point to point. Now you have 6 halves.

6. On a spare piece of release paper, place 2 different-color tree halves together, slightly overlapping the edges down the middle, and fuse-tack them together. Make 3 trees. Leave them on the release paper.

7. Repeat Steps 1–6 for each of Sections 2–5. Refer to the quilt photo (page 66) and diagram (page 69) to make the number and color of trees needed.

Assemble leaves on release paper.

Making the tree trunks

Make all the trunks as described in the following steps, using the red fabric. Trim them to fit each section.

1. Remove the release paper from the red fabric. Using a wavy blade in your rotary cutter, cut on the bias 17 strips, each at least 9″ long. (This will create enough strips for all the trees in the quilt.) The strip width should taper from ½″ at one end to almost nothing at the opposite end.

Cut tapered strips for tree trunks.

2. Place a trunk down the center of each tree and fuse-tack in place.

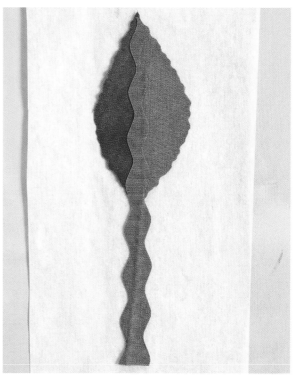

Lay trunks along treetop centers.

3. Peel the trees off the release paper, and position them on top of Section 1, referring to the quilt photo (page 66) and the assembly diagram (page 72). (Leave Section 1 on a piece of release paper.) Fuse-tack them in place.

4. Repeat Steps 1–3 to add the trees and tree trunks to Sections 2–5.

Assembling the center rectangle

1. Align a large piece of release paper over the craft-paper background pattern. Place Section 1 on it in the proper position.

2. Place Section 2 on the release paper, and slightly overlap Section 1 on top of it. Fuse-tack these in place.

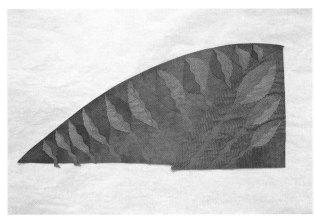

Section 1 slightly overlaps Section 2.

3. Place the combined Sections 3 and 4 on a separate piece of release paper, and align them so there is a small overlap. Trim the top edge smooth and fuse-tack them together.

4. Place the combined Sections 3 and 4 on the release paper with Sections 1 and 2, tucking the bottom edge under Section 2. Fuse-tack this in place.

5. Place Section 5 on the release paper, tucking the bottom edge under Sections 3 and 4. Fuse-tack this in place.

6. Remove the whole center rectangle from the release paper, and trim the 4 sides even. It should measure 15″ × 18″.

Making the border

Now it's time to cut and assemble the border pieces.

1. Using a regular rotary blade, cut 4 strips 4″ × 27″ from the border fabric.

2. Place the squared-up center section back on a piece of release paper, and slip the top and bottom border strips under the edges of the center rectangle, with the rectangle's edges slightly overlapping. Fuse-tack them together, and trim the border ends even with the center section.

3. Repeat Steps 1 and 2 for the side borders.

Making the border trees and tree trunks

You will use 3 fabrics (Gradation Steps 10–12) to create the 32 trees in the border.

1. On a piece of release paper, use a black Sharpie marker to trace around the border tree pattern (page 72).

2. You will make 11 trees from each color of fabric. (You will not use 1 of the trees.) Place the release paper marked side down on the fused side of the fabric, and press with a hot, dry iron to transfer the tree pattern (Step 2, page 43). Repeat 10 times for each fabric.

3. With a deckle blade in your rotary cutter, cut out the tree shapes slightly outside the lines.

4. From the same 3 fabrics, cut out 32 tree trunks using a deckle blade in your rotary cutter. For each tree, cut on the bias a tapering strip 4″ long. The strip width should taper from ¼″ wide at one end to almost nothing at the opposite end.

5. On a piece of release paper, place a contrasting-color fabric stem down the center of each border tree and fuse-tack it in place.

6. Place the trees around the border as shown in the assembly diagram below; 6 trees go on the top and bottom border pieces, 8 on each side section, and 1 angled at each corner. Trim the trunks flush with the inside border edge.

7. Fuse the trees to the border.

8. Place the whole unit on top of the pressed backing unit, and fuse-tack in place. Pin at the 4 corners.

Assembly diagram

Machine quilting the quilt

I first stitched in-the-ditch around all the straight "seams" with the feed dogs up, using a straight stitch in matching thread. Next, I stitched down the center of each trunk with a contrasting thread to give them a little pizzazz. I added stippling to all the background areas with matching thread, but you can leave them plain if you prefer. I machine quilted my name in a tree on the border.

To finish your quilt, refer to Making a Fused Binding (pages 46–47) and Making a Pleated Quilt Sleeve (pages 48–49). Add a label, as described on page 49, if you wish.

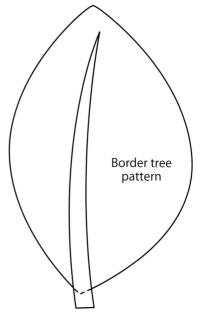

Border tree pattern

Border tree pattern

FINISHED SIZE: 27″ × 37″

Made and machine quilted by Frieda Anderson

I love trees and their leaves, and I am fascinated by the way the leaves change color all through their "lives." They are never just green or red or brown. They shift in color as they age—from the beginning of spring, when they are almost mint green, to the end of their lives, when they are dirt brown and metallic gray.

This spectacular quilt was inspired by those changing colors. The design allows you to show off the full range of your beautiful hand-dyed fabrics: it uses all three values of both Bright Color and Warm Color gradations. Each of the seven rows of striped leaves is created from a different but related set of colors.

Note

This project goes faster if you keep extra release paper at hand on your ironing surface.

Materials

All fabrics are dyed with Dharma Trading dyes. If you are dyeing fabrics specifically for this project, dye fat quarters of the colors listed. (The backing will require a larger amount.) The amounts of fabric given below are the minimum amounts needed to make this quilt.

For leaves:
Piece 9″ × 10½″ from each of all 3 values (light, medium, and dark) of Steps 3–9 (orange, red-orange, red, red-violet, violet, blue-violet, and blue) in both gradations (Bright and Warm) (42 pieces total)

For borders:
Piece at least 9″ × 16″ from each dark value of Step 12 (yellow-green) in both gradations (Bright and Warm) (2 pieces total)

Piece at least 6″ × 16″ from each light value of Step 12 (yellow-green) in both gradations (Bright and Warm) (2 pieces total)

Piece at least 6″ × 9″ from each light value of Steps 2 (yellow-orange) and 3 (orange) in the Bright gradation (2 pieces total)

Piece at least 9″ × 16″ from each medium value of Steps 2 (yellow-orange) and 3 (orange) in the Bright gradation (2 pieces total)

For border squares:
Piece at least 3″ × 14″ from each of the dark values of Steps 2, 4, and 10 (yellow-orange, red-orange, blue-green) in the Bright gradation

Piece at least 3″ × 14″ from each of the dark values of Steps 2, 3, 10, and 11 (yellow-orange, orange, blue-green, and green) in the Warm gradation

Fat quarter of fabric for binding

29″ × 39″ piece of fabric for backing

29″ × 39″ piece of flat cotton batting

8 yards of fusible web

Note

You will also need a large sheet of craft paper or newsprint at least 18″ × 28″, a large rotary cutter to cut through 6 layers of fabric at once, and a chalk marker.

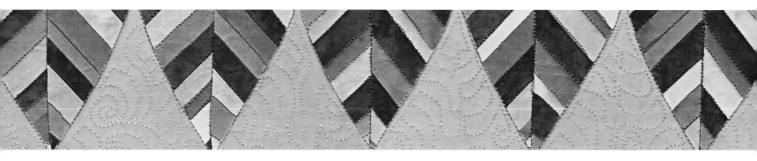

Preparing the fabrics

Apply fusible web to the backs of the fabrics, as described in Fusing Basics (pages 41–42). Apply web to the leaf fabrics in the following manner: Cut 21 strips of fusible web 10″ × 17″. Cut these in half to measure 8½″ × 10″ and apply to each of the fabrics.

Let the fabric and fusible web cool. As you use each piece of fabric, remove and save the release paper.

Layer the batting with the backing fabric, pressing them together to get a nice, smooth sandwich. Set this aside.

Creating the master diagram and leaf pattern

You will make 2 half-leaf patterns, which you will use and reuse to make all the leaves.

1. On a large sheet of craft paper or newsprint, draw the center section. It measures 17½″ × 28″.

2. Measure up from the bottom 7″ and draw a line across the rectangle.

Measure up every 3½″ and draw a line. This will be your guide when laying out the leaves.

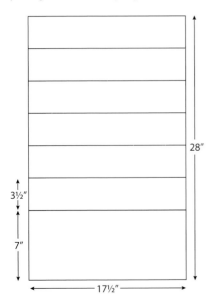

Diagram for leaf placement

3. Trace the leaf pattern twice, onto 2 separate pieces of release paper. Cut 1 leaf shape in half lengthwise to create 2 halves. Mark the left side "Lip" and the right side "Right," and draw a 45° line on each half as shown. You will use the remaining whole leaf as a guide for lining up the 2 finished leaf halves to create the whole leaf.

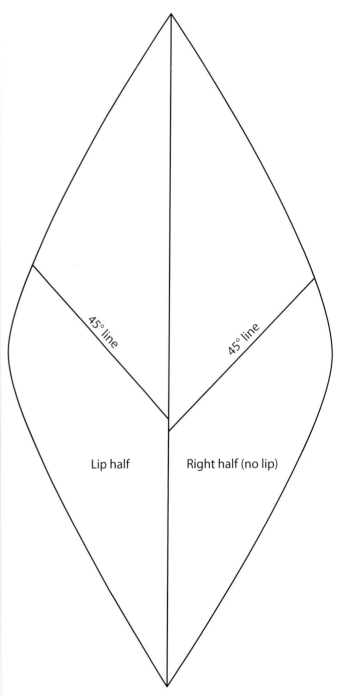

Leaf pattern; make 2 copies.

Making the leaves

1. The first row, or set, of leaves is made using all 6 of the orange (Gradation Step 3) fabrics. Remove the release paper from the prepared fabrics, and stack all 6, fused side up, on your rotary mat. Using your largest rotary cutter and a ruler, cut on the bias 6 strips of fabric 10½″ long in various widths from ⅜″ to ⅝″, for a total of 36 strips.

Cut strips on bias.

2. On your ironing surface, sort all the strips on release paper into similar piles by color.

3. Working on the release paper, begin making striped units. Place a strip of fabric fused side down on the paper, and set another strip of a different color and/or width next to and slightly overlapping the top of the first one. Fuse-tack together.

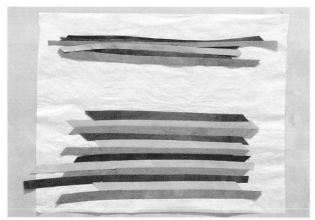

Sort strips on release paper and combine strips to make striped unit.

4. Continue in this fashion until you have at least 12 strips of fabric fused together to make a piece approximately 6″ × 10½″. Let this cool, peel the fabric off the release paper, and set it aside. Repeat this process to make 3 more sets of orange gradations. Vary the way you lay the fabrics together—you don't want each set to look the same.

5. Lay the striped units fused side up on your ironing surface. Place each of the 2 paper half-leaf patterns diagonally on the striped unit, using your drawn diagonal 45° line as a guide to line up the stripes. Keep the marked sides of the patterns face up. Remember to keep each half with the word "LIP" and the word "RIGHT" on the top side.

Lay leaf patterns on fused side of striped units.

6. Place an extra piece of release paper on top to protect your iron, and fuse-tack the leaf patterns in place.

Place extra release paper on top of leaf patterns, and fuse-tack in place.

7. Peel up the top release paper after it has cooled. On your cutting mat, use a regular-blade rotary cutter to cut out the Right leaf half exactly on the pattern edges. Cut out the Lip half, leaving a ¼″ lip on the long, straight side and cutting exactly on the curved edge. Peel off the patterns and save them to reuse.

Lip half of leaf cut out with ¼″ lip

8. Cut out 5 or 6 sets of leaves. (I like to make an extra one so I have one to discard—in case.) After cutting out as many leaves as you can from the original strip sets, use leftovers to create new sets by fuse-tacking the parts together. *Note:* Do not place all the leaf halves neatly in a row on a strip set. You can save fabric by doing this, but one side of your leaves will all look exactly the same, without any color variation.

9. Place a pair of finished leaf halves on top of the whole-leaf paper pattern, overlapping the right half on top of the ¼″ lip of the left half. Fuse-tack them together. Trim the tips with extra-sharp embroidery scissors. Repeat this step 4 more times to create 5 leaves in each color. Remember to make sure all the stripes in the leaves are

pointing down in the same direction. Now you have made the first set (row) of leaves.

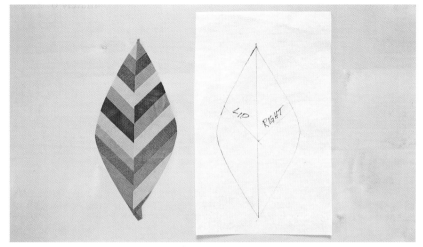

Use release-paper pattern to line up leaf halves.

10. Repeat Steps 1 through 9 to make a set of leaves in each Gradation Step. *Note:* For rows 2, 4, and 6 (red-orange, red, blue-violet), you will not fuse-tack 2 of the leaf halves together because they will be used as half leaves at the ends of the rows.

Laying out the rows

1. Place a piece of release paper over the diagram of the center section, and line up the first row of leaves, one right next to the other. Use the drawn lines as a guide to keep the leaves straight. Fuse-tack the leaves in place.

2. As you make the rest of the leaves, place them in their rows on the release paper. Place the Gradation Step 4 (red-orange) fabric leaves underneath the Step 3 (orange) fabric leaves, and line up the top tips with the drawn line of the diagram. Fuse-tack them in place. Repeat this process for the Step 5–9 fabric leaves.

Lay out rows of leaves on top of release paper over craft-paper diagram.

3. When all the leaves are lined up and in place, press the entire center section together on top of the release paper. Let it cool, and peel it off the paper.

4. Place the center section on your rotary mat, and trim the left and right sides even.

Making the border

1. Trim the fusible-backed border background fabrics to 8½″ × 15″ for the top and bottom borders, 5½″ × 14½″ for the lower side borders, and 5½″ × 7½″ for the upper side borders.

2. Place the border pieces around the center section. Slightly overlap the center section on top of the edge of each border fabric, and slightly overlap the border fabrics where they come together to form "seams." Refer to the assembly diagram on page 78. You will trim to square up the outer edges of the border later.

3. Fuse-tack together the borders and the main section on release paper. You will have to use several pieces of release paper or a large pressing sheet.

4. For the border squares, apply a 3″ × 15″ strip of fusible web to each of the border square fabrics. Remove the release paper, and cut 2″ × 15″ strips from each of these fabrics. Cut these into 2″ squares. You will need 36 squares total.

Cut 40 squares for border.

5. Using a ruler and chalk marker, draw a line on the border 2″ out from the edge of each side of the main section. Use this chalk line to lay out the 2″ squares on-point. There will be 8 squares along the top and bottom

and 12 squares along each side. Once they are all in place, fuse them to the border with the release paper in place underneath. Let this cool.

6. Peel the quilt off the release paper, and trim to square it up to measure 27″ × 37″.

7. Place the whole unit on top of the pressed backing unit, and fuse-tack in place. Pin at the 4 corners.

Assembly diagram

Quilting the quilt

I started stitching this quilt by stitching in-the-ditch along the lines down the centers of the leaves. Then I free-motion stitched all the leaf veins between the strips, stitched in-the-ditch around all the border squares, and free-motion stitched a squiggly line down the center of each square. In the border, I stitched a modified Baptist Fan design.

To finish your quilt, refer to Making a Fused Binding (pages 46–47) and Making a Pleated Quilt Sleeve (pages 48–49). Add a label, as described on page 49, if you wish.

resources

PROCION MX DYES

Dharma Trading Company
Offers many different dyes, including Procion MX type, Procion H type, Inko dyes, acid dyes, and many types of paints. Carries fabric for dyeing and is the best source of clothing blanks. Also carries auxiliary products such as Bubble Jet Set and Synthrapol. Very helpful catalog and website.

800-542-5227 or 415-456-7657

www.dharmatrading.com

PRO Chemical & Dye
Dyeing supplies of all kinds

Orders: 800-228-9393

Technical support: 508-676-3838

www.prochemical.com

Jacquard Products
Procion MX dyes and other dyes, paints, and auxiliaries

800-442-0455

www.jacquardproducts.com

Dick Blick Art Materials
800-828-4548

www.dickblick.com

Jerry's Artarama catalog
P.O. Box 58638J

Raleigh, NC 27658-8638

800-827-8478

FABRICS

Testfabrics, Inc.
570-603-0432

www.testfabrics.com

Kaufman Fabrics
PFD and many other fabrics. Check the website for retailers.

You can order Kona PFD white cotton fabric in 50-yard bolts.

800-877-2066

www.robertkaufman.com

Exotic Silks
800-965-0712

www.exoticsilks.com

BOOKS ABOUT DYEING

Blumenthal, Betsy, and Kathryn Kreider, *Hands on Dyeing*. Interweave Press, 1988.

Broughton, Kate, *Textile Dyeing: The Step-By-Step Guide and Showcase*. Quarry Books, 2001.

Deighan, Helen, *Dyeing in Plastic Bags: No Mess–No Fuss–Just Great Colours!* Crossways Patch, 2001.

Dunnewold. Jane, *Complex Cloth: A Comprehensive Guide to Surface Design*. Martingale and Company, 1996.

Johnston, Ann, *Color by Accident and Color by Design*. www.annjohnston.net

Mori, Joyce, and Cynthia Myerberg, *Dyeing to Quilt: Quick, Direct Dye Methods for Quilt Makers*. McGraw-Hill, 1997.

Widger, Katy, *The New Color Wheel Fabric Dyeing*. www.katywidger.com.

Wilcox, Michael, B*lue and Yellow Don't Make Green*. School of Color, 2002. (This is a book about water-color painting, but it has good color formulas.)

About the Author

I made my first quilt when I was in high school. I have always made things, and I love the process of creating. In college I majored in art history and minored in ceramics, but I returned to fiber because it was more satisfying. I can't remember when I didn't sew. For years my focus was designing and making clothing. All that changed in 1992, however, when I was in fashion design and realized that all I wanted to do was make quilts. I have been designing and making original quilts ever since.

I find each step of quiltmaking, from the beginning to the end, a real challenge. It is hard to say what part I like best. I love the pure creativity involved in conceiving and designing a new quilt. I love to piece and I love to fuse. I have found that by fusing smaller pieces, I can work out design issues. Then I like to make a bigger, bolder statement and piece the same quilt in a large format. Most of my work is machine quilted and nature inspired. Everyday I walk in a little wood near my home with my dog, George. Much of what I see there appears in my work.

I discovered hand dyeing fabric 16 years ago, and I now work almost exclusively with my own hand dyed cottons and silks. I love the dye process, and I particularly enjoy seeing the colors emerge from the wet fabric.

Great Titles *from* C&T PUBLISHING

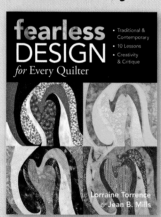   

Available at your local retailer or **www.ctpub.com** or **800-284-1114**

For a list of other fine books from C&T Publishing, ask for a free catalog:

C&T PUBLISHING, INC.
P.O. Box 1456
Lafayette, CA 94549
800-284-1114 | Email: ctinfo@ctpub.com
Website: www.ctpub.com

C&T Publishing's professional photography services are now available to the public. Visit us at www.ctmediaservices.com.

Tips and Techniques can be found at www.ctpub.com > Consumer Resources > Quiltmaking Basics: Tips & Techniques for Quiltmaking & More

For quilting supplies:

COTTON PATCH
1025 Brown Ave.
Lafayette, CA 94549
Store: 925-284-1177 | Email: CottonPa@aol.com
Mail order: 925-283-7883 | Website: www.quiltusa.com

Note: Fabrics used in the quilts shown may not be currently available, as fabric manufacturers keep most fabrics in print for only a short time.